Paleo Diet:

Exactly What Your Body Needs!

Physicians, biochemists, nutritionists, and other researchers are starting to come around to the benefits of ancestral nutrition, and people who adopt a Paleo-like approach to eating are reporting significant improvements in their general health, body composition, and energy levels. Most importantly, there is evidence that folks who eat this way are reducing their risks of numerous diseases and disorders that are associated with the Standard American Diet (S.A.D.).

The **Paleo diet** is the healthiest way you can eat because it is the only nutritional approach that works with your genetics to help you stay lean, healthy, and energetic! Research in biology, biochemistry, Ophthalmology, Dermatology and many other disciplines indicate that it is our modern diet, full of refined foods, trans fats, and sugar, that is at the root of degenerative diseases such as obesity, cancer, diabetes, heart disease, Parkinson's, Alzheimer's, depression and infertility. – Robb Wolf.

TABLE OF CONTENTS

INTRODUCTION

The Paleo Diet (Paleolithic), which is also called the "Caveman" or "Stone Age" diet, centers around the idea that if we eat like our ancestors did 10,000 years ago, we will be healthier, lose weight and curb disease. A swift and concise definition of the Paleo diet is — "if the cavemen did not eat it then, you should not either," says Academy Spokesperson Jim White, RDN, and ACSM/HFS. The foods in this context means foods that can be hunted, fished or gathered: eggs, fish, poultry, meat, veggies, roots, berries, shellfish, and fruits. Meaning, there will be no grains, no dairy, no legumes (beans or peas), no sugar, and no salt. Why paleo diet? "According to proponents, our bodies are genetically predisposed to eat this way. They blame the agricultural revolution and the addition of grains, legumes, and dairy to the human diet for the onset of chronic disease (obesity, heart disease and diabetes)," says White.

The word "diet" in paleo diet seems to mislead people into believing that paleo diet is all about a temporary weight loss program, but it is not. Rather, it is based on the notion that for optimal health, modern human should go back to eating completely unprocessed foods that are more healthful than harmful to our bodies.

When people hear the word caveman, they tend to freak out as they say it sounds like weird fad diet, but by the time you finish this book, you will see that the story is entirely different.

Over the past 200,000 years, humans have biologically adapted best to whole foods; plants, meats, seafood—all of them packed with the nutrients our bodies evolved to thrive on. Then, in about merely 10,000 years ago (a tiny fraction of our evolutionary history), agriculture came on the scene, and there simply has not been enough time and evolutionary pressure for humans to completely adapt to eating modern foods like wheat, sugar, chemically processed vegetable and seed oils, and other "Neolithic" foods. One thing we must sincerely address is that it is not a coincidence that many modern diseases of civilization including autoimmune disorders, cardiovascular disease, type 2 diabetes, and rampant obesity have accompanied the global spread of industrialized food. That is why the Paleo approach emphasizes returning to a more historical approach to eating.

This approach to eating encourages the addition of more fruits and vegetables and cutting out added sugar and sodium, which aligns with the 2010 Dietary Guidelines for Americans. The combination of plant foods and a diet rich in protein can help control blood sugar, regulate blood pressure, contribute to weight loss and prevent Type 2 diabetes, says White.

People also complain that the Paleo diet might be hard to sustain. I agree with them that it might be a bit arduous given that we live in a society where it is not possible to eat exactly as our ancestors ate. For example, wild game is not readily available, as most of the meat we consume has been domesticated. In addition, the plant food we eat has been processed rather than grown and gathered in the wild. While strict conformity is not realistic, it is possible to modify the plan, eating only wild caught fish, grass-fed meat and organic fruits and vegetables.

Paleo diet comes as good news for people that say they do not like keeping track of how much they have eaten or obsess about how many grams of a particular nutrient they have had. The point is that you do not have to count calories if you can expand your horizons and remove certain foods from your diet. Paleo diet offers the way out of diet worries.

One of the greatest deviations away from our ancestral diet is the amounts and types of fat found in modern grain feed animals versus the amounts and types of fats found in grass fed or wild meat, fowl, and fish. It was observed that wild meat is remarkably lean, and has relatively little amounts of saturated fats, while supplying significant amounts of beneficial omega-3 fats such as EPA and DHA.

This book shall look extensively into paleo diet: the history, the health benefit, the problems, examples of turnaround achievements using paleo diet, some recipes, and what professionals have found out and their remarks. The history will help us see how modern human diet has changed, compared to the ancient human diet. The health benefit will account for the reasons why paleo diet is better than modern diet: detailing the health issues that accompany modern diets, the problems will discuss the challenges faced on the paleo journey, and the recipes shall be to help you out on how to fix some quick and easy paleo diet. What professionals say will be to buttress all that has been said.

CHAPTER ONE

HISTORY OF THE PALEO DIET

Defining Paleo diet

It is imperative to define the term "paleo diet" in order to clear the misconceptions about paleo diet and hence set the course for what you are about to learn.

"Paleo" is not a literal term; in the 21st century, humans simply do not eat food that is thousands of years old. Therefore, mimicry is an essential element. To the authors of The Paleolithic Prescription, mimicry is limited to nutritional levels; As long as it is numerically balanced, people could eat whatever they wanted. Today, however, most advocates of the Paleo Diet attempt not to only mimic the nutrients, but also the foods that contain them. Under this mindset, "modern" or post-agricultural foods are excluded; a Paleolithic diet means consuming the very foods that might have been available to cavemen themselves. Like humans, these foods are also living organisms and therefore subject to evolution. "Diet" has taken on a remarkable double meaning. On one hand, diet is defined as what is eaten: the sum of food consumed by a person, no matter what it is or the time it is eaten. On the other hand, diet can also be understood in the context of going on a diet: eating either less food or different food altogether. Weight loss seems to be the most commonly desired outcome, but anything from religious or ethical beliefs to medical problems prompt people to go on diets of the second meaning. Each one differs from the other in just about every comparable way (including legitimacy among doctors and dieticians, prompting the term "fad diet") but whether it is the Atkins Diet or the grapefruit diet; it is entirely a modern idea. Before the elimination of food scarcity in many parts of the world, diet was not a choice but rather the outcome itself. The never-ending quest for enough calories to survive meant that people would eat anything they could get their hands on and the only weight loss connected to diet came in the form of starvation. Therefore, the Paleo Diet falls somewhere in the middle. Assuming evolutionary accuracy for now, it fits the first definition because it is both what Paleolithic humans ate and modern humans mimicking them eat today. This mimicry is a choice with anticipated outcomes, however, the Paleo Diet also fits the second definition of diet. Such ambiguity has prompted people like Loren Cordain to adopt the term "program of eating" to describe the Paleo Diet; like many other vocal adherents, Cordain argues for its place as a long-term lifestyle and not a quick-fix, or an on-and-off solution. After this brief exposition about the meaning of paleo diet, let us now go into the history to see how these foods, which are also living organisms, have evolved over time.

THE HISTORY

The notion of a nutritional plan purposely centered on the presumed diets of Paleolithic ancestors is comparatively recent; its popularity span is less than fifty years. In order to wholly comprehend the idea's broader origins, however, we must travel back to the turn of the 20th century. Environmental historian Roderick Nash suggests that this era ushered the rise of a "wilderness cult," in which certain environmentally inclined members of the public embraced a return to primitivism amongst a progressively modern existence.

Some environmental organizations such as the Sierra Club, instituted by John Muir in 1892, pledged to explore, enjoy, and protect the wild places of the earth. The Boy Scouts of America, instituted in 1910, echoed these conservationist goals and urged America's urban youth to experience nature in its most primeval form. Possibly the most recognizable supporter of the movement was 26th President of the United States of America, Theodore "Teddy" Roosevelt, who in addition to founding the hunting-conservationist Boone and Crocket Club in 1887, sternly advocated for the creation and expansion of the

National Park Service. Roosevelt's commitment to wilderness preserves echoed his argument that embracing the "strenuous life" would lead to ultimate triumph for nature-toughened Americans as the new century dawned.

Likely, no one in the early 1900s held Teddy Roosevelt's so-called "strenuous life" in as high regard as Joseph Knowles. Joseph Knowles is a 44-year -old professional illustrator from Maine who set off into the New England wilderness on August 10, 1913, to conduct a self-described "experiment." Naked and entirely without supplies, Knowles hoped not only to survive for two months without human contact but also to share his journey with the public through a periodic tree-bark correspondences to the Boston Post. Named the "Primitive Man" by the newspaper, Knowles' wilderness diet consisted of berries, trout, and various small game; he even claimed to have killed a bear with only a crude club in the experiment's second week. Knowles used animal hides as cloths and fashioned sandals from strips of moist tree bark.

When he emerged from the forest on October 4, the tan and thickly bearded Voyager received a hero's welcome from the citizens of Boston. His subsequent memoir, *Alone in the Wilderness*, sold some 30,000 copies, and the "primitive man" became a household name for a brief period following the book's publication. Despite questions of the experiment's validity (a rival newspaper claimed that Knowles purchased his famous bearskin pelt and spent much of his journey drinking beer in a friend's cabin), Knowles swore that the wilderness journey substantially improved his overall health.Among his claims were that he lost weight but gained muscle, his complexion improved, his digestion became "perfect," and he acquired the ability to lift "over a thousand pounds" with his legs alone. Flaws aside, Knowles' journey established him as one of the first Americans to openly (though temporarily) reject modernity for a primitive lifestyle.

Going down the twentieth century, Joseph Knowles' visions of a healthy nation living like cavemen gained little popularity. Industrialism and scientific advances led to mass-produced, readily available food, and many people found themselves living increasingly sedentary lifestyles. Strength training for athletes was uncommon through the 1950s (many feared that lifting weights or other anaerobic exercise made participants "muscle bound"), and like dietary science, kinesiology was a virtually nonexistent academic field.

Born in 1937, Dr. Arthur De Vany was a product of this era. De Vany received his Ph.D. from UCLA in 1970 and became a motion picture economist, but his true passion was for exercise science. He often spent his workdays observing the exercise routines of Hollywood stunt actors, many of whom lifted heavy weights and scheduled their meals around grueling film shoots. De Vany used these observations to create his "evolutionary fitness regimen," designed to simulate the physical and dietary habits of human hunter-gatherer ancestors. The program called for periods of intermittent fasting followed by high-intensity cardiovascular exercise and regular compound weightlifting. De Vany's routine follows the generalized reasoning that hunter-gatherers lived meal-to-meal and often had to chase down prey before dragging or carrying it back to the place of consumption. While the plan initially failed to make much of an impact in both scientific and fitness circles, Arthur De Vany stands as a pioneer of applying evolutionary thinking to fitness and diet. In 2010, his book The New Evolution Diet: What Our Paleolithic Ancestors Can Teach Us about Weight Loss, Fitness and Aging updated his proposed evolutionary fitness plan to include nutritional information published in the last two decades.

Despite only brushing the surface of Paleolithic nutrition, Joseph Knowles and Arthur De Vany framed the public relationship between evolutionary history and modern science. The explicit suggestion that a diet mimicking the Paleolithic era could lead to health benefits, however, was first popularized in 1975 by gastroenterologist Dr. Walter

Voegtlin. Dr. Voegtlin's self-published book, The Stone Age Diet: Based on In-Depth Studies of Human Ecology and the Diet of Man remains a polarizing advancement. On one hand, it represents the first time that a medical doctor publicly advocated an ancestral diet based on scientific evidence. Voegtlin's radical suggestion that humans are chiefly carnivorous, however, was met with skepticism from both the public and fellow physicians. Despite longstanding evidence of plant food consumption in sources like archaeological digs and cave art, Voegtlin claimed that human ancestors were "exclusively flesh-eaters."

Furthermore, he advocated replacing sugar with the artificial sweetener Sucaryl. Sucaryl was invented in 1937 and banned by the U.S. Food & Drug Administration in 1969 after it was linked to a myriad of health problems, mostly cancer of the bladder.

The Stone Age Diet was fatally flawed, but it was a revolutionary work that exposed the clear lack of popular and scientific understanding of human ancestral diets. Another monumental dietary product of the 1970s replaced the commercial and scientific failure of Walter Voegtlin's Stone Age Diet: Dietary Guidelines for Americans. This joint publication by the Department of Health and Human Services (HHS) and Department of Agriculture (USDA) had its first publication in 1980, but it started as the 1977 brainchild of the Senate Select Committee on Nutrition and Human Needs.

Led by Senator George McGovern, the committee used extensive data from both scientists and industry groups to propose five core dietary recommendations for Americans:

• Increase carbohydrate intake to 55% -60% of calories

• Reduce dietary fat intake to no more than 30% of calories, with a reduction in intake of saturated fat, and recommended approximately equivalent distributions among saturated, polyunsaturated, and monounsaturated fats to meet the 30% target decrease cholesterol intake to 300mg per day

• Reduce sugar intake to 15% of calories

• Reduce salt intake to 3g per day

Despite widespread media publicity, the recommendations made by the Senate were met with considerable debate and controversy from industry groups (particularly cattle, dairy, egg, and sugar producers) and some members of the scientific community, who questioned the specificity of the recommended numbers and accused the committee of catering to profitable lobby organizations. The Senate responded by establishing a scientific review panel, but the first published edition of Dietary Guidelines for Americans in 1980 contained few changes from the 1977 Senate report. In 1990, Congress authorized the HHS and USDA to produce an updated version of Dietary Guidelines every five years; the most recent report which is from 2010 is far more detailed than its predecessors, but the recommended macronutrient proportions remain consistent with the levels introduced in 1977.

One of the scientists who took a critical look at both Dietary Guidelines for Americans and The Stone Age Diet is Melvin Konner, a medical doctor and professor of Anthropology, Neuroscience, and Behavioral Biology at Emory University in Atlanta. In 1985, he and fellow physician Stanley Boyd Eaton attracted significant scientific and medical attention to the concept of Paleolithic nutrition through their article publication in The New England Journal of Medicine. Entitled "Paleolithic Nutrition: A Consideration of Its Nature and Current Implications." Eaton and Konner's article suggests that differences between ancestral diets and those in modern industrialized countries have "significant implications for health," including a possible connection to the new rise in illnesses like coronary heart disease, hypertension, diabetes, and certain types of cancer.

Furthermore, they contend that the development of agriculture has apparently had a "minimal influence" on our genes.

Eaton and Konner used a dietary sample of 58 current hunter-gatherer groups, which are not only varied by their geographic locations but also by a number of daily calories they obtained from animal foods. None of the sample populations utilized agriculture, because these groups acquired their food in a way that resembled Paleolithic humans. Eaton and Konner consequently argued that their diets provide an estimate on what human are "genetically programmed to eat, digest, and metabolize."

Melvin Konner and Stanley Boyd Eaton's research findings differed considerably from the nutritional recommendations in Dietary Guidelines for Americans. Instead of meat and fish, vegetables and fruit, milk and other dairy products, breads and cereals (the "four basic food groups" listed by Dietary Guidelines as "foods choices that should be emphasized"), Konner and Eaton found that pre-agricultural hunter-gatherers derived all of their nutrients from the first two groups alone. "They apparently consumed cereal grains rarely, if at all," the scientists concluded, "and they had no dairy foods whatsoever."

While the sample groups that Konner and Eaton studied varied widely in their ratios of animal to vegetable food

14

consumption (some groups ate as much as 90% animal foods, and others as little as 15%) , the authors used the average ratio of 35% animal foods and 65% plant foods to estimate nutritional characteristics.

From this, they concluded that approximately 45% of a "typical" late Paleolithic diet is made up of carbohydrates, 34% of protein, and 21% of fat, a large difference from the modern Senate recommendations of 58, 12, and 30 percent respectively.

The authors of "Paleolithic Nutrition" noted that estimating ancestral diets was "intellectually satisfying and a heuristically valuable reference standard," but beyond their musings on "modern" health problems, their work was devoid of any explicit advocacy towards eating like a hunter-gatherer.

The article did cause a stir within the medical community, however, several of Eaton and Konner's colleagues urged the pair to introduce their findings to the public. They obliged, and in 1988, the two men (along with Konner's wife Marjorie Shostak, an anthropologist specializing in hunter-gatherer women) published The Paleolithic Prescription: A Program of Diet & Exercise and a Design for Living. Instead of simply implying a connection between modern diets and "modern" diseases, The Paleolithic Prescription urged readers to improve their health by adopting the same nutrient proportions as were present in average Paleolithic diets. Interestingly enough, the book did not exclude foods that were absent prior to agriculture; as long as the 45/34/21 macronutrient ratio was approximately met, followers of the program could still consume foods like whole grain bread, rice, potatoes, and milk.

Modern understanding of Paleolithic nutrition drastically increased in the 1970s and 1980s, but the movement still lacked widespread recognition and tangible evidence of health benefits. These shortcomings were reduced significantly in the last decade of the 20th century, mainly due to the Kitava Study. Named after a small Pacific island in the Trobriand Archipelago (officially part of Papua New Guinea), the Kitava Study comprised a series of scientific surveys started in 1989 by Swedish medical doctor and Lund University professor Staffan Lindeberg. In the Study's first survey, Lindeberg and his colleagues interviewed 213 adult members of the island's indigenous population about their dietary habits and health concerns. In addition to recording their heart activity using an electrocardiogram (ECG), they found that the islanders maintained an active, subsistence-based lifestyle uninfluenced by western dietary habits; their diets consisted almost exclusively of fish, tubers, fruit, vegetables, and coconut.

Furthermore, the survey revealed no reported cases of stroke, sudden death unrelated to accidents or homicide, or angina pectoris (heart -related chest pain). In other words, the Kitava natives appeared to live in a society absent of stroke and coronary heart disease.

Subsequent surveys contributing to the Kitava Study in the mid-1990s revealed more about the diet consumption and health outcomes of native islanders. Despite deriving less than 0.2% of their caloric intake from typical "modern" foods (including but not limited to bread, cereal grains, dairy, processed sugar, and alcohol), Kitava researchers encountered no cases of malnutrition or famine; most natives even consumed more vitamins, minerals, and soluble fiber than the scientists had observed in a typical Swedish diet.

Both salt and fat were consumed in relatively small quantities (the latter made up approximately 20% of total caloric intake) on the island. Saturated fat, however, made up a higher percentage of total fat intake in Kitava than in Sweden, a statistic explained by the Islanders' elevated levels of coconut consumption.

The scientists noted that like stroke and heart disease, obesity and hypertension were virtually nonexistent in Kitava, as were any signs of dementia or memory loss among the island's 138 residents between the ages of 60 and 95.

Perhaps, the most puzzling aspect of the early Kitava research was the average lifespan on the island: just 45 years. Why were the Islanders, who seemed to be extraordinary healthy, dying at such a young age? The answers were two folds. Firstly, the leading causes of death were completely unrelated to diet and ironically are considered "primitive" or preventable in many Western societies: infections (primarily malaria), pregnancy complications, and accidents topped the list.

Secondly, Kitava's disproportionately high rate of infant mortality significantly dragged down the average figure; Lindeberg estimated that the post-adulthood rate much more closely resembled his native Sweden's.

Following the groundbreaking results of the Kitava Study in the 1990s, both academic and commercial interest in Paleolithic nutrition has dramatically increased. As scientists continued to research the health effects and evolutionary connections of the human diet, the early 2000s saw a dramatic surge in commercial book and Internet advocacy of hunter-gather nutrition. It was also in the 2000s that the first widespread usage of the term "Paleo Diet" emerged. The name's ownership is a subject of great debate, but most credit Dr. Loren Cordain for its introduction into the public vocabulary. Currently a Professor of Health and Exercise Science at Colorado State University, Cordain received his Ph.D. in Health from the

University of Utah in 1981. His website, ThePaleoDiet.com, proclaims him "the world's leading expert on Paleolithic Diets and founder of the Paleo movement."

Beyond the obvious bias in that statement, Cordain's resumé checks out: he has authored and co-authored more than 100 peer-reviewed articles appearing in publications like the American Journal of Clinical Nutrition and the World Review of Nutrition and Dietetics, including several collaborations with Stanley Boyd Eaton and Staffan Lindeberg. Two of Cordain's books, The Paleo Diet, published in 2001, and The Paleo Diet for Athletes, published in 2012, have reached the New York Times' bestseller list and bridged much of the gap between academic and popular interest in Paleolithic eating.

Unlike Konner and Eaton's groundbreaking attempt to identify a "typical" Paleolithic diet, Loren Cordain's research primarily focused on forming and analyzing a contemporary experimental diet (hereby referred to as "Cordain's Paleo Diet") based on what he calls "Paleolithic food groups."

Commonly available modern foods are the diet's focus elements, while processed foods, cereal grains, and dairy products are excluded entirely excluded. Using a similar analysis of hunter-gatherer societies as his predecessors, Cordain estimated a higher percentage of animal foods

(55%) than Konner and Eaton's 35%. As a result, his macronutrient proportions differed as well; Cordain's Paleo Diet calls for just 23% carbohydrates, 38% protein, and a full 39% fat.

Despite these incongruities, Cordain supports that his diet is rich in many areas where a contemporary Western diet is deficient, including vitamin, antioxidant, and dietary fiber intake. Cordain argues that increased animal-food and fat-consumption percentages in Cordain's Paleo Diet would not lead to unfavorable increases in blood lipid profiles (an indicator of both weight gain and cardiac distress) due to the hypolipidemic effect of increased dietary protein and relatively low carbohydrate and saturated fat levels. It would be a nearly impossible task to credit all the major players in the modern Paleo Diet movement, mainly because new ones are constantly emerging. In 2013, the term "Paleo Diet" was the most-searched dietary topic on Google, and some estimates put the number of American Paleo adherents between one million and three million, or around 1% of the country's population.

In conclusion, beyond the scholarly interest and output between the 1970s and the present, thousands of commercial Paleo-focused avenues (from websites, blogs and message boards to cookbooks and magazines to simple word-of-mouth discussions and personal dietary experiments), have made impacts that are beyond doubts on the identity (or many identities) and direction of the Paleo Diet. This book is another in-depth work on the paleo diet.

Paleo Diet

CHAPTER TWO

HEALTH BENEFITS OF PALEO DIET

People always ask, what are the benefits of being on paleo diets? I am glad to bring the following influences to your knowledge.

RESEARCHES ON DIETS INFLUENCE

There are essentially two different pathways for evaluating the nutritional "effectiveness" of any diet, including the Paleo Diet: macro-level comparative studies of the diet as a whole, and component-based discussions evaluating issues like nutrient composition, elimination of grains and dairy, the healthiness of fąt consumption, et cetera.

Four clinical, peer-reviewed studies (three utilizing human test subjects and the fourth utilizing domesticated pigs) form the extent of Paleo Diet comparative research.

In 2006, Swedish researchers published a study of the long-term effects of the Paleo Diet on risk factors for three "diseases of affluence" (type-2 diabetes, obesity, and cardiovascular disease) in domestic pigs. Over a period of fifteen months, 24 piglets were split into two diet groups: the first consumed cereal based swine feed and the second consumed a Paleolithic Diet; both groups maintained the same caloric intake. At the study's outset, the scientists tested for glucose levels, insulin response to glucose consumption, levels of C-reactive protein (a physiologic marker of subclinical inflammation), and blood pressure. They found that in addition to the Paleo Diet group weighing 22% less, and containing 43% subcutaneous fat thickness at mid-sternum, blood pressure was 13% lower. Insulin response to injected glucose was 47% higher, which means C-reactive protein was 82% lower, and no significant differences was seen in fasting glucose levels among the two groups.

In 2008, another team of Swedish scientists published a study assessing the effects of a short-term switch to the Paleo Diet among already healthy human volunteers. For three weeks, twenty subjects free of observable health issues who are self-identified as healthy ate only Paleo Diet foods until they were full in a non-controlled caloric manner. At the study's outset, the scientists tested for changes in weight, body mass index (BMI), waist circumference, blood pressure, and caloric and nutrient intakes. Fourteen of the twenty subjects fulfilled the study, and complete the dietary assessment (i.e. nutrient intake levels) was available for six. The scientists found that mean weight decreased by 2.3 kilograms, mean body mass index (BMI) decreased by 0.8 points, mean waist circumference decreased by 0.5 centimeters, and mean blood pressure decreased by 3 millimeters of mercury. Caloric intake decreased by 36%, while fat composition generally decreased and antioxidant prevalence increased generally. Calcium consumption decreased, which the scientists found unfavorable. Overall, the scientists concluded that some favorable effects were shown, but that further studies, including those with a control group, were needed.

A team of American researchers from the San Francisco School of Medicine published The third macro-level study of the Paleo Diet in 2009. The scientists tested nine non-obese sedentary healthy volunteer who are non-obese; these participants consumed their normal diets for three days, three "ramp-up" diets of increasing potassium and fiber for seven days, and a Paleolithic diet for ten days. Caloric intake was held consistent to prevent day-to-day weight loss. At the end of the three days baseline diet period and the –ten days Paleolithic diet period, the scientists tested for blood pressure, insulin sensitivity, blood lipid concentrations, total cholesterol, and brachial artery reactivity (a measure of blood flow effectiveness). Compared with the baseline diet period, the Paleolithic diet period brought significant reductions in blood pressure, significant increases in insulin sensitivity, significant reductions in both total cholesterol and blood lipids, and improved circulatory status; in each of these measured variables, either eight or all nine volunteers had nearly identical responses. The scientists concluded that even short-term consumption of a Paleolithic Diet improves metabolic and physiologic status based on these criteria.

In 2009, Swedish researchers published the fourth comparative study of the Paleo Diet. The scientists tested thirteen patients with type-2 diabetes; in a random order, the subjects consumed a Paleolithic Diet for a three-month period and a "Diabetes Diet" (high in cereals and dairy, low in animal protein and total fat) for another. At the end of each period, the subjects were tested for cardiovascular risk factors including weight change, waist circumference, blood lipids, blood pressure, and levels of high-density lipoprotein (HDL) or "good" cholesterol. Compared to the Diabetes Diet period, the scientists found that the Paleolithic Diet period brought on lower mean values of weight, waist circumference, blood pressure, and blood lipids, as well as higher mean values of HDL cholesterol. From these outcomes, the scientists concluded that the Paleolithic Diet improved glycemic control and several cardiovascular risk factors compared to the Diabetes Diet in patients with type-2 diabetes.

Despite these successful outcomes in clinical studies, the Paleo Diet is still widely discouraged by nutritionists and commercial media outlets. The former tends to oppose the elimination of entire food groups (dairy, grains, and foods with added sugar) for a balanced diet that meets nutritional requirements. According to Joy Dubost, a registered dietitian and a spokesperson for the Academy of Nutrition and Dietetics. He said, " In theory this may seem like a sensible diet, particularly when removing sugar and salt, it has eliminated several food groups like dairy and grains, which provide essential nutrients, such as calcium, vitamin D, magnesium and phosphorus in dairy and B vitamins, fiber and antioxidants in grains. Legumes also provide an excellent source of protein with little fat and lower calories while providing essential nutrients and fiber."

While Dubost's factual analysis is correct, her logic inherently fails to discount the Paleo Diet; yes, foods are eliminated, but the "essential nutrients" listed can all also be found in the Paleo Diet. Other nutritionists, like New York University nutrition professor Lisa Sassoon, are even more critical: "There's no real research behind it either. And it eliminates things that do have research behind them: grains, beans, and low -fat dairy." Perhaps Sassoon should expand her knowledge of research to include both the Paleo Diet studies and those displaying possible negative health effects of the three food groups she cited.

The opinions of Joy Dubost and Lisa Sassoon was frustrating for proponents of the paleo diet, but the frustration only increased upon uncovering the following: in its 2014 rankings of "Best Diets Overall," the U.S. News and World Report classified the Paleo Diet as tied at dead last out of 32 options.

According to the nutritionists and "health experts" who served as panelists for the rankings, a top -rated diet had to be easy to follow, nutritious, and safe and effective for weight loss and against diabetes and heart disease. The Report's highest ranked diet was the government-endorsed Dietary Approaches to Stop Hypertension (DASH) diet, a balanced choice that instructs followers to "emphasize the foods you have always been told to eat:" fruits, vegetables, whole grains, lean protein, and low-fat dairy. From a typical nutritionist's perspective, the DASH diet (if eaten in a balanced way) seems like an incredibly well researched choice that is safe to be recommended.

The fact that the DASH diet was ranked considerably above the Paleo Diet on the "Best Diets Overall" list was not a surprise. In addition, it is not what got most paleo diet proponents frustrated. Despite the report's claims that there is "no way to tell," if someone would lose weight on the Paleo Diet (the report failed to include simple discussions of caloric intake), and that by shunning food groups, "you're at risk of missing out on a lot of nutrients." They ranked the Slim-Fast Diet a full eighteen places ahead of the Paleo Diet, tied as the thirteenth-best diet choice.

The Slim-Fast Diet advocates its followers to consume just 1,200 calories per day: one 500-calorie self-prepared meal, two Slim-Fast meal-replacement shakes or bars, and three snacks, "half a banana or a Slim-Fast snack bar."

Without putting into consideration how hungry one would be if they ate only 1,200 calories of mostly liquid foods day after day (good luck not eating that other half of the banana), the Slim-Fast Diet is entirely based on what nutritionists apparently fear the most: avoiding whole food groups for a substitute. That substitute, a French Vanilla Slim-Fast meal replacement shake, contains 18 grams of sugar (its third ingredient) in addition to things like acesulfame potassium (a "nonnutritive sweetener"), cellulose gel, and citric acid among its forty -plus ingredients. Who needs things like the Paleo Diet's natural fruits and vegetables or satiating lean meats when the Slim -Fast Diet is a much better option?

Despite these prominent displays of anti-Paleo Diet sentiments, a handful of nutritionists are willing to consider it a viable alternative. Conversely, leading Paleo Diet advocates have admitted that elements of a more contemporary Western diet can work as well. According to New York-based nutritionist Jennifer Andrus, the food groups eliminated from the Paleo Diet "can be" (not are) part of a healthy diet. However, more pressing issues are at hand: "I think processed food deserves the criticism, but probably not because we haven't evolved; more likely because we eat too much of it and most of it is nutritionally void."

Heather Neal, another dietician, and self -described "former hater of the Paleo Diet," admits that she changed her tune after failing to lose weight or feel better eating a conventional Western diet: "The dairy tore up my stomach. The wheat fogged my brain,I think the Paleo Diet is a great way to get people to open up their minds to a new way of eating."

None other than Loren Cordain mirrors this logic on the other side of things: "Cereal grains obviously can be included in moderate amounts in the diets of most people without any noticeable, deleterious health effects," Cordain noted in 1999, adding, "When combined with a variety of both animal-and plant-based foods, grains provide a cheap and plentiful caloric source."

Compiling the voices and stories of ordinary people who switched from a contemporary Western Diet to the Paleo Diet is no small task. However, those outcomes only exist in humongous numbers. One of the largest resources for uncovering Paleo Diet stories from "ordinary people" is the social media/news-based interactive online community Reddit, which has a section (or "subreddit" as they are known) where more than 64,000 people read, ask questions, and contribute stories, pictures, and recipes related to the Paleo Diet.

Researchers of the Paleo Diet consider Reddit to have the most useful and eye-opening non-academic content of any Internet resource, and I highly encourage both ardent skeptics and Paleo devotees to discover its firsthand accounts in a cautious but open-minded manner.

GENERAL HEALTH AND NUTRITIONAL ADVANTAGES OF PALEO DIET

It Promotes Healthy Cells

One of the facts people failed to realize is that every cell in human body is made-up of both saturated and unsaturated fat, and our cells depend on a healthy balance of the two to send messages in and out properly. The paleo diet naturally provides a perfect balance of fats because it suggests both in healthy amounts while other diets limit one or the other.

Enhances Healthy Brain

One of the best sources of protein and fat suggested by the paleo diet is gotten from cold-water fish: ideally wild-caught salmon. Salmon fat is very rich in omega 3 fatty acids which is absent in the average modern diet. This is something to be taken serious given that omega 3 fatty acids contain DHA, which is known to be good for the eyes, heart, and most importantly for the development of the brain and its function. Other sources of omega 3 fatty acids are found in pasture-raised meats and eggs.

Gives the Body More Muscle, Less Fat

The Paleo diet relies heavily on animal flesh and with it comes healthy protein. This protein is highly anabolic and it is used for building new cells like muscle mass. Metabolism works better in proportion to the muscles we have in our body. This is because muscles require energy to move and in order to move bigger muscles; we have to store more energy in them. This allows your body to send energy to muscle cells instead of fat cells. By increasing muscle cells and shrinking fat cells (through a healthy paleo diet), any extra energy will be transported to glycogen in our muscles against triglycerides in our fat cells.

To further buttress this, scientist says that due to genetics, some people have higher metabolic rates than others, but muscle mass is an important factor to consider in determining your BMR. Muscle is more active and energy demanding than fat, therefore, if you have a higher percentage of muscle compared to fat, you will have a higher BMR.

Result in Better Gut Health

Sugar, manufactured fats and other processed junk all result in inflammation within your intestinal tract. Unfortunately, when too much-processed foods is combined with lot of stress, it can lead to what is called "leaky gut syndrome": which is when your intestinal walls are breached and things that are not supposed to leave the tunnel end up leaking out. With no doubt, we want to keep the food we eat in our digestive tract until it is ready to be transported to the cells. Scientists found out that "The bolus of blood sugar that accompanies a meal or snack of highly refined carbohydrates (white bread, white rice, French fries, sugar-laden soda, etc.) increases levels of inflammatory messengers called cytokines." Given that stress is what we live with on a day-to-day basis in this modern period, paleo diet's lower carbohydrate component is hence important for us to achieve better gut health.

Maintains Cycle of Life

The paleo diet proposes that we should eat pasture-raised meats and eggs. This means that the animals are truly able to wander in the grass for their whole lives. Ideally, cows and chickens will roam the pasture together as this creates synergy. In nature, chickens will follow cows around and eat the larvae and bugs found under the cow pies. Naturally, the cow pie will get broken up which fertilizes the grass which then provides food for the cow. This process continues as a cycle hence preserving the natural process. This natural diet is great for the animals but it also serves you a long list of nutrients when you eat them due to their healthy diet. It is the circle of life at its finest.

Note that scientists have discovered that "Eggs from pastured hens can contain as much as 10 times more omega-3s than eggs from factory hens"

It is rich in Vitamins & Minerals

The paleo diet advises eating the rainbow (that is eating vegetables of different colors), Vegetables are a large part of the diet and it is recommended to get a variety of veggies depending on the seasons. The different colors of veggies are dependent on the nutrients they contain! By eating the rainbow, you ensure you get all your vitamins.

Scientists have established the fact that "Vegetables are important sources of many nutrients, including potassium, dietary fiber, folate (folic acid), vitamin A, and vitamin C."

It limits the level of Fructose in the body

The human body digests fructose differently than other carbs, and the paleo diet recognizes this unlike most or almost all of the modern diets. Because of this, the paleo diet suggests that we should limit and strategically choose the perfect fruit for the job. Skip the banana and eat a kiwi instead. Unless you know what you are doing, try not to take more than 2-3 pieces of fruit per day.

Scientific research have proved that "...chronically high consumption of fructose in rodents leads to hepatic and extra hepatic insulin resistance, obesity, type 2 diabetes mellitus, and high blood pressure"

Aids Better Digestion and Absorption

The paleo diet recommends eating foods that we have adapted the ability to digest over thousands of years. There are no queries whether or not you can tolerate starch or grass-fed beef. Our ancestors survived and thrived off these foods. If you are having digestion problems, I would greatly advise you to try a strict paleo diet for about thirty days and I guaranteed you would feel better.

Scientists said, "Fermented foods, ranging from sauerkraut to yogurt, are increasingly being seen as a boon to the gut—and in turn to benefits not only for digestive health but possibly also for allergies and even weight loss"

Greatly reduces Allergies

The paleo diet put forward that you reduce as much as possible the foods known to be allergens to certain societies. Some people that have problems digesting seeds (grain) and dairy which is why the paleo diet recommends that you remove these foods from your diet at least for a month (unless the milk is raw). People often bash the paleo diet because we do not eat "whole grains" and this could not be further from the truth. The truth is simply that grains are not the best tool for the job, so we avoid them most of the time, but not all the time. If you are an athlete, you probably should be eating a cup of oats every now and then. Paleo diet is not about hating certain diets, it just aspires to help people be the best they can be, and that starts with choosing quality foods.

According to scientists, "Reported raw milk consumption was indirectly associated to asthma"

It Reduces Inflammation

Cardiovascular disease has been linked to inflammation with research referring to it, as may be the leading factor for the disease. The great and very much welcomed thing about the paleo diet is that many of the foods are anti-inflammatory, so we will be minimizing the risk. Its great focus on omega 3 fatty acids is one of the reasons the diet is so anti-inflammatory. Pasture-raised animals have a much better ratio of omega 3 to 6 ratios and the other veggies and herbs encouraged with the paleo diet will help as well.

Scientists say "Research shows that omega-3 fatty acids reduce inflammation and may help lower risk of chronic diseases such as heart disease, cancer, and arthritis"

Gives More Energy

In the last decade, energy drinks have become so much popular and this make people like me wonder why it has become so prevalent. You are mostly likely to agree with me that it is because everybody's diet sucks. For example, a typical American breakfast consists of a sugar coffee matched with a muffin or bagel with cream cheese. Not only will this eventually lead to type 2 diabetes and insulin resistance, it will not even keep one satiated. With the paleo diet, one strategically chooses the right foods for any occasion.

Scientists said, "Eating foods with a low glycemic index (whose sugars are absorbed slowly) may help you avoid the lag in energy that typically occurs after eating quickly absorbed sugars or refined starches"

Helps in Weight Loss

The paleo diet is designed to be a low carb diet. By simply removing processed foods, we will drastically reduce our carb intake to fuel weight loss. By limiting carbs to around workout times, we will avoid unwanted fat gain, which is often caused by these excess carbs.

Pertaining to this, Scientists say that many of the foods that increase disease risk (chief among them, refined grains and sugary drinks) are also factors in weight gain"

Increased Insulin Sensitivity

If every day for six months, one had ice cream with every meal, I guarantee you that eventually one would start hating ice cream. Whenever a bowl of ice cream is placed for the person, it would be kindly rejected. This same thing is true for our body. When you constantly feed your body cheap, sugary foods, the body desensitizes itself to them because it does not want or need them.

Your body only needs enough energy, and when you reach that threshold, your cells reject the fuel and store it as fat. If this continues for too long, you will develop insulin sensitivity which means your body will be incapable of recognizing when your cells are full or not.

Scientists say, "Even short-term consumption of a Paleolithic type diet improves BP and glucose tolerance, decreases insulin secretion, increases insulin sensitivity and improves lipid profiles without weight loss in healthy sedentary humans"

Declining Risk of Disease

My point is not to say that the paleo diet is perfect and it is of course not, but the focus is to avoid foods that can potentially harm your health. The paleo diet makes it easy to avoid crap foods by giving you a simple blueprint; only eat what a caveman would be able to eat. While this is not perfect, it will ensure you eat whole foods and limit your risk for disease by avoiding the foods known to cause them. By following a Paleo diet, you are inevitably eating more anti-inflammatory foods and cutting out many of the foods that known to cause inflammation. You are also eating more foods that contain antioxidants and phytonutrients which are always making the news because of scientific evidence that points to them helping to ward off or battle back cancer, as well as prevent heart disease. You are also naturally avoiding many of the culprits responsible for disease and illness, like fast food and junk food, so you get a more natural version of yourself and open the doors for healing and well-being.

What Scientists have to say about this is that "All populations appear to develop diseases of civilization if they consume Western foods and have sedentary lifestyles. Therefore, it seems wise for modern-day humans to remember their evolutionary heritage, to increase their intake of vegetables and fruits, and to decrease their intake of animal fats and domesticated grains. The Paleolithic diet might be the best antidote to the unhealthy Western diet"

Shrink Those Fat Cells

Many people fail to realize that fat cells shrink and expand based on our diet. Note that a lean person does not have less fat cells they simply have smaller cells. In order to keep your fat cells tiny you must choose healthy fats and limit your carb intake; all things the paleo diet suggests. Healthy fats are tightly packed together within our cells and are readily available for energy when you are insulin sensitive (as explained above). It is basic synergy at work here; the paleo diet naturally provides the foods that will add muscle and keep our insulin sensitive, thereby, ensuring your fat cells stay compact. The avoidance of carbs will ensure your cells stay healthy and able to burn that fat.

Scientists say that "As triglycerides are stored within a cell, the fat blob inside the cell expands, increasing the cell's diameter. If enough fat cells in a body region enlarge this way, that part of the body begins to look fat"

Balances Blood Glucose Levels

Because you are avoiding refined sugar, it is easier to avoid spikes in your blood glucose levels, and helps us avoid feelings of fatigue we get when sugar level is too low. Note that if you are diabetic, you will want to check with your doctor to see if they approve of this diet plan. If you are simply trying to avoid getting diabetes, this will be a better diet choice than an average typical fare. In the same vein, if you are not concerned about diabetes and just want to feel better or lose weight, monitoring your blood sugar levels is a great way to do that.

Leaner Muscles

Because this diet plan relies so much on meat, you will be getting a fair amount of protein to feed your muscles. It helps to promote a leaner physique, and can even help with muscle growth if you engage in weightlifting while on it. When you consider the physique of Stone Age man, they did not really have a lot of excess baggage in the form of many fat and underdeveloped muscles. They were lean, mean, sabretooth tiger battling machines, and this sort of efficient physique still helps in our modern world. With a leaner body structure, you will be able to handle life's challenges better, including the stresses that occur with a busy 21st century lifestyle.

It helps one Avoid Wheat and Gluten

When on paleo diet, you are inevitably cutting out wheat products, which gets rid of the gluten, so in essence you are following a gluten-free diet at the same time. There is plenty of evidence that suggests that gluten is difficult for the digestive system and for weight gain, even for those that do not have Celiac disease, or do not have a sensitivity to gluten. However, cutting out these food items that have been shown to contribute to larger midsections and sluggish digestion, you immediately improve your body makeup and start to feel better all around.

Keeps You Feeling Fuller Longer

Most diets keep us in a constant state of hunger, but with a Paleo diet we are focused on feeling full and feeling good, which means that it is easier to follow, and has lower instances of diet crashes and cheating because you are encouraged to eat when you feel hungry. It also contains a fair amount of healthy fats, which helps us keep that full feeling and avoid food cravings. If one is eating the right mix of proteins from meat, as well as vegetables that help you to feel full, and fruits that give just the right amount of fiber and carbohydrates, you will have no problem making it from meal to meal. When Paleo-approved foods are combined in the right way, we are getting a well-balanced meal with protein, carb, and vegetable, and are of course gotten from all-natural sources. This is the way to feel more energized and at the top of your game without having to recourse to energy drinks, caffeinated beverages, and other means to get you through the day. Moreover, unlike other diets that rely on a reduced amount of calories, the Paleo diet allows you to eat until you feel full, and to eat whenever you feel hungry, so you do not run the risk of running low on fuel when you really need it.

No Counting is Required

Unlike a diet that has one watching points, or counting how many carbs you have in a day, the Paleo diet is simple and easy to follow. The lack of rules and limitations on how much you can have each day makes it interesting and easy to stick to the plan. By not having to limit yourself, you do not get your brain fighting against you or rejecting the plan resulting in self-sabotage. You are able to eat like a human should eat, and how we did eat before things got so complicated.

Helps us Sleep Better

By cutting out the chemicals and additives in typical food sources, you will then see that your body naturally gets tired at night. This happens because other chemicals from food do not override the serotonin that your brain releases as a pointer that it is time to sleep. When you start to feel sleepy, you should sleep. You might discover that you are getting tired earlier at night, and that you feel energized and ready to wake up earlier in the morning. This is your body getting in tune with the circadian rhythm, just as prehistoric man was.

Helps us Avoid Processed Foods and fast foods

When you cut out processed foods, you are cutting out many synthetic chemicals that have just come about in the last century and that the body just has not adapted to yet. You may be startled by just how many foods get the "do not consume" because of the processing involved, and how much you used to rely on these foods on a day-to-day basis. It may be a bit difficult to give up dairy products, or products that come out of boxes. There may be a period of both physical and psychological adjustment as you reach toward a more natural way of living, and you notice just how embedded you've become in modern conveniences. The fast food industry is notorious at making headlines for how bad their food is. By going

Paleo, you instantly cut out all fast food because they, cavemen didn't have McDonald's. The health benefits of not eating fast food.

Cuts out Junk Food

An end has come to maxim and relaxing in front of the TV with a bag of Ruffles. There is no room for the junk food when we are on Paleo, and this alone means that we are improving our well-being, and only channeling our fund in to getting food that helps us, not harm you. This is fast food's at-home cousin and one item that one will be glad he/she gave up, if not straightaway but down the road when we start looking in the mirror and liking what we see. It is likewise advantageous for our food budget, as these items can be pricey to pay for the large ad budgets it takes to get people to buy them. Spend that savings on organic meats and vegetables and you will be doing yourself a big service.

Slashes out Empty Carbs and Calories

Some other things that are out when we are doing paleo are sodas and other sugary beverages because there is nothing prehistoric about them. Pure water and maybe some herbal teas was all Stone Age man had, so you are going to have to cut out Pepsi, energy drinks, juices, and other beverages that are sugar laden and full of chemicals.

For many people, just cutting out these empty carb sources leads to weight loss, feeling better, and having more sustained energy levels through the day with no crashes. With Paleo, every carb and calorie we take in serves a purpose, and serves our body in a positive way.

Provides Detoxing Effects

By ending the intake of many things that bring us down which include: Trans fats, MSG, caffeine, refined sugar, gluten and more, we are giving our body rest. By getting more antioxidants from the fruit we will be eating, and more phytonutrients and fiber from the vegetables we will be eating, we will be purging our body of built-up waste and accumulation. Overall, this provides a detoxifying effect to the body, and many Paleo followers have reported that they feel lighter and more clear headed after several weeks. The good thing about it is that it does not entail going to extremes like fasting or drinking nothing but juice, we get to eat meals like normal, so it could be said to be a very lazy detox.

Keeps Things Simple

Many people are tired of always pondering on what to eat, what to make for a meal, what is good for them and what is not (I surely belong to this group), Paleo can keep things really simple and make it so your whole life does not revolve around food anymore. We will be eating to live instead of living to eat, and that can free up a lot of mental effort on our part. One is likely to be surprised by what a burden this takes off us, and how much time it really frees up. We do not have to constantly be thinking about our next meal, we can have things set up so that we know exactly what we will be eating on a day-to-day and weekly basis, and we can start to put our focus on matters that are more important.

Increases our Intake of Fruits and Vegetables

In today's world, many people like most Americans struggle to meet daily intake of fruits and veggies. This is not astonishing since for most, these are regarded as "health foods" and make it onto the dinner plate as a compulsory side dish to make a meal healthier. Nevertheless, with Paleo, they are given more of a starring role along with meat, so we are going to be depending on them more than we were previously. The bottom layer of the standard food pyramid will be wiped out and replaced with meats and vegetables and healthy fats as your base layer, sprinkling in some fruits to keep your taste buds in the game.

Increases Your Intake of Healthy Fats

It is truly kind of difficult to get our head around healthy fats actually helping to burn fat, but that is just what they do, so it is good to get our fair share of healthy fats each day. The Paleo plan makes them an important part of our day so that we do not have to worry if we are getting enough. These fats help you feel fuller for a longer time, which reduces food cravings and helps you stick to eating at mealtime only. However, remember if you feel hungry, you can totally eat as long as you are eating foods that are on the approved foods list.

Effortless Weight Loss

Without having to do anything else but switching over to a Paleo way of eating, many will notice that the weight just starts coming off. This is because in addition to eating a meal that is more natural, we are cutting out lot of foods that are unnatural. When we shift our energy from having to lose weight and feeling guilty about the foods we are eating, we will notice that eating becomes interesting again. An interesting occurrence is that the more fun we have and the better we feel, the more we will want to stick to a program that makes us feel that way, and the easier it is to lose weight. If we are constantly resenting our diet plan and craving things we cannot have, it is a recipe for disaster. It is psychological.

PALEO DIET AND DIABETES AND OTHER LIFESTYLE DISEASES

Diabetes is sometimes called a "lifestyle disease," which means that it is caused by lifestyle factors like diet and exercise, rather than a particular germ or gene. It is most of the time (though not always) associated with other lifestyle diseases like obesity, high cholesterol, and high blood pressure, because the same kinds of lifestyle patterns tend to cause more than one of those problems. In this aspect, I will not be going in to what diabetes is (as it is not what we set out to do and will not want to be distracted by it), I will rather place my focus solely on the roles paleo diet play in the control or treatment of diabetes (type 1, type 2 and gestational diabetes). The modern Paleo diet was essentially designed to provide solution to exactly that problem. It is really about treating lifestyle diseases like diabetes and metabolic diseases underlying obesity (which in many ways is a symptom of hormonal problems). When it comes to diabetes, the goal of Paleo is to address all the factors that contribute to insulin resistance. **It is not limited to carbs, and it is not even limited to diet.**

Many recent research supports that low-carb diets can be very effective for Type 2 diabetes. Some research shows that low-carb diets may be particularly effective for people with insulin resistance. But it's worth noting that "low-carb" in these studies can be up to 40% carbs by calories, which is medium-high carb by Paleo standards (giving room for a couple of potatoes every day).

These improvements are not coming from a straight diet of steak and lettuce. Some people might do very well on that – a very low-carb ketogenic diet can also be great for diabetes. A study found that, in teenagers, a low-calorie diet with 40-45% carbs was just as good as a diet with 55-60% carbs if the subjects exercised and took metformin.

I guess you are wondering; what about the fat? The problem with fat is that when eaten together with lot of refined carbs, fat really is very fattening. In addition, the wrong type of fat is reasonably dangerous: trans fats are inflammatory and do contribute to metabolic problems. Paleo diet also solves this problem as it eliminates certain foods.

PALEO DIET AND CARDIOVASCULAR DISEASES

The effect of a Paleolithic diet on a variety of metabolic risk factors for cardiovascular disease in an uncontrolled trial was reported in August 2009 in the *European Journal of Clinical Nutrition*. Compared with the usual diet, nine sedentary subjects receiving the intervention diet experienced

(a) Significant reductions in blood pressure

(b) improved arterial distensibility

(c) Significant reduction in plasma insulin versus time in the area under the curve during oral glucose tolerance testing and

(d) Significant reductions in total cholesterol, low-density lipoproteins, and triglycerides

The authors concluded that even short-term consumption of a Paleolithic type diet improves blood pressure and glucose tolerance, decreases insulin secretion, increases insulin sensitivity, and improves lipid profiles without weight loss in healthy sedentary humans

FEW STUDIES ON INFLUENCE OF PALEO DIET VERSUS OTHER DIETS

► **Paleolithic nutrition improves plasma lipid concentrations of hypercholesterolemic adults to a greater extent than traditional heart-healthy dietary recommendations.**

Heart healthy diet recommendations are meant to be the gold standard when it comes to decreasing the cholesterol of hypercholesterolemic adults. Their entire model revolves around reducing blood lipids through diet (and maybe a few prescription drugs), so you would think that the official AHA diet would thrash the supposedly unproven, untested, and dangerously meat-centric and grain-deficient paleo-type diet when it comes to cholesterol numbers. However, this is not so.

In this study, subjects with high cholesterol used four months on the sanctioned AHA diet followed by four months on a paleo diet. The AHA diet phase emphasized lots of fruits and vegetables, little to no salt, fish twice a week, tons of whole grains, no more than 7% of calories from saturated fat and no more than 300 mg of cholesterol a day. During this portion of the trial, subjects failed to hit any of the desired blood lipid changes. Neither HDL, triglycerides, LDL, nor total cholesterol got any better or worse on the AHA diet.

The paleo phase emphasized lean animal protein, fruits, vegetables, eggs, and nuts. Dairy, legumes, and grains were all restricted. During this part of the trial, traditional cholesterol markers improved across the board. LDL, TC, triglycerides went down, and HDL went up. Moreover, during the paleo phase, patients lost more weight and ate fewer calories (without being instructed to do so).

Note that a paleo-type diet with unlimited eggs, zero grains and legumes and dairy, and no strict caloric limit is not just safe but leads to better blood lipids, more weight loss, and greater calorie reduction than an official AHA heart-healthy diet that limits eggs, dietary cholesterol, saturated fat, and places strict limits on total calories.

▶**Marked improvement in carbohydrate and lipid metabolism in diabetic Australian aborigines after temporary reversion to traditional lifestyle.**

This is one of the earliest-known paleo diet studies, so early that the diet was called a "reversion to traditional lifestyle" rather than paleolithic. In it, ten diabetic, middle-aged, overweight Australian aborigines were instructed to live as hunter-gatherers for seven weeks, only eating what they were able to collect or hunt on their traditional homelands. Their base "city diet", the diet that got them diabetic and overweight, consisted of flour, sugar, rice, soda pop, alcohol, powdered milk, cheap fatty meat, potatoes, onions, and various fresh produce. Their new diet looked very different: Beef, kangaroo, crocodile, fish, turtle, crawdads, yams, honey, and figs. Fat content of the diet ran between 13%-40%. Protein content ranged from 50% to 80%, and carb content ran between the ranges of 5% to 33%. Overall, 64% of the diet came from animal foods and average caloric intake was 1200 per day.

In a period of seven weeks, the subjects had lost an average of 8 kilograms (17.6 lbs.), fasting glucose had gone from diabetic to non-diabetic, postprandial glucose had improved, fasting insulin levels had plummeted, and triglycerides had dropped.

Note that some combination of increased energy expenditure (although the study author estimated that activity levels were higher than normal, but not dramatically so), reduced caloric intake, elimination of processed industrial foods, and consumption of healthy traditional foods caused the massive improvements in diabetic markers.

▶ **Paleolithic and Mediterranean diet pattern scores and risk of incident, sporadic colorectal adenomas.**

The Mediterranean diet is typically mentioned for its advantageous effect on colorectal cancer. It is low in red meat (a popular whipping boy in colorectal cancer circles), high in extra virgin olive oil with potent antioxidant effects, rich in whole grains whose fiber is supposed to stave off colon cancer, and features sufficient amounts of red wine whose polyphenols exert protective effects against colon carcinogenesis. Paleo diets, meanwhile, eliminate whole grains and place no limit on red meat. In addition, while they usually allow both red wine and olive oil, they do not emphasize any of the two. So when a team of researchers found that high adherence to paleo diet principles was just as protective against colon cancer as adherence to Mediterranean diet principles, some people were surprised. I was not surprised.

Note that assuming this epidemiological research indicates a true causal relationship between diet and colon cancer risk, we can draw a few tentative guesses. You do not need whole grains to have a healthy colon. You can eat meat and enjoy a healthy colon. You probably still need ample amounts of prebiotic fibre (and there is evidence that prebiotics are important mediators of the effect dietary red meat has on colon cancer risk), but it does not have to come from grains and legumes; fruit and vegetables and tubers are perfectly adequate.

▶**Long term effect of a Paleolithic-type diet in obese postmenopausal women: two years randomized trial.**

The term "Long-term" here is relative, and we would all love to see 30 or 40 years long randomized trials, but those are cost prohibitive. A randomized dietary trial lasting two years is incredibly rare and deserves our full attention. So, what did they find out?

Subjects were divided into two groups. One followed standard paleo diet, the other followed a high-carb, low-fat Nordic Nutrition Recommendations diet (fairly standard "eat healthy whole grains, avoid artery clogging saturated fat" approach, although with higher fat

allowances than most heart healthy diets in the US). The group following paleo lost more body fat, especially abdominal fat, at 6, 12, and 18 months. They also had more sustained drops in triglycerides after two years, and their blood pressure improved to a greater degree.

The weight loss and biomarker improvements were accompanied by dietary shifts typical of Primal/paleo diets: reduced carb intake, increased protein intake, increased monounsaturated fat intake, reduced omega-6 intake, increased omega-3 intake.

Note that it is safe. Two years is usually enough time for some worrying trends to appear. None did, though the obese women who lost so much body fat at six months, twelve months, and eighteen months on the paleo diet had pretty much flat lined at 24 months, allowing the Nordic diet group to catch up to them. This was probably because they did not stick with the diet, as indicated by their difficulty maintaining the elevated protein intake normally associated with paleo in these studies. For any diet to continue working, you have to do it diligently.

▶**A Paleolithic diet is more satisfying per calorie than a Mediterranean-like diet in individuals with ischemic heart disease.**

Participants in this diet were overweight with big bellies, either glucose intolerance or outright diabetes, and a confirmed diagnosis of ischemic heart disease. In other words, they consisted of the typical people who really need to change their diets. They were randomized to receive either a paleo-like diet or a Mediterranean-like diet.

The paleo diet was based on meat, fish, eggs, nuts, vegetables, fruit, and root vegetables. While the Mediterranean diet was based on whole grains, fish, low-fat dairy, fruits, and vegetables.

Both groups reported high satiation from their respective diets, but the paleo group consumed fewer daily calories and smaller meals to achieve it. While the Mediterranean group needed over 1800 calories a day to feel full, the paleo group ate a hair under 1400 to achieve the same level of satiation. In addition, that is without eating any more protein (well known for its powerful induction of satiety). Calorie for calorie, the paleo food was simply more filling.

Note that there is something about eating plants and animals while avoiding grains and other processed junk that improves satiation, beyond the added protein that normally accompanies a lower-carb Primal way of eating.

CHAPTER THREE

PROBLEMS ENCOUNTERED ON PALEO DIET JOURNEY

You may have just got on the train of your Paleo journey and it seems a never-ending challenge changing from your old lifestyle to your new. You could also be a veteran to the diet, but still find yourself at one time or the other picking away at a fresh loaf of bread, or nibbling on some sweets. Perhaps, even worse, you feel like you are doing everything right, yet you fail to see the results in weight loss, increased energy or improved general health. These are stories that people often tell; hence, this chapter will address these challenges and I hope it will make your life a little easier, or in the very least assist you kick those bad habits to the curb.

Some people do not experience these challenges when switching from their former lifestyle to the paleo lifestyle, but I guess many would say that they were only fortunate not to experience too many of these trials and tribulations when they made such lifestyle changes. Perhaps the fact that some out of these people were in a rapid downward spiral, willing to try anything to feel better and that they armed themselves with wealth of information, would be the reason why. Having said that, any new adjustment to our lives there will usually be some obstacle knocking at our door and waiting at every corner we get around. Unfortunately, I believe you know and agree with the fact that change is not often something easy to achieve. Otherwise, the Paleo community would have been a lot bigger than it is today. This transition in your life will certainly test your abilities to stay committed and determined, as many other transitions in other areas of life will. It is no easy feat, but I can assure you that the rewards are like none other and you will find out eventually that it is worth whatever price paid. Some people thrive on challenges, while many others choose to run away from them.

For those of us who have experienced great success on Paleo, it can be difficult to comprehend why one would do anything less, but this can be quite understood: It is easier to keep doing the same thing, and a lifestyle change is rarely easy. For someone who has not put a lot of thought into what it means to be Paleo, it can be quite stressful. The idea of eliminating foods that you have consumed your whole life on a very frequent basis and not fully understanding what will fill that gap is scary. Furthermore, without enough information, how is one to comprehend that eating grains, refined sugar and vegetable seeds oil are so toxic to your health while they often do not seem to be causing any issues. Without taking it one-step further and learning about what being Paleo means to your overall health, it seems much easier to bail out. Unfortunately, this is what happens plenty of times.

You know I keep wandering why so many individuals fail to stick to the diet or stick to it but failed to see the great results that we are talking. It would good to make it clear that it can be different for everyone and will likely be, but when we consider the Paleo community, there are certainly some common reasons for failure. Come with me as I talk at length about many of these problems (because it is possible I do not cover it all but I believe that every other problem borders on the ones I will talk about here or they are outshoots), and learn to change your lifestyle in a much easier manner, not because rules are changing but because of the wealth of information you will gather to arm yourself against these challenges.

The technical reasons

In many cases, these "technical reasons" are the reasons why some people fail to achieve the proper health results on the diet even though they stick to it and feel like they do it correctly. Let me also emphasize that there is a lot of conflicting information out there when it comes to Paleo, and some people are led to make changes based on some wrong information that are not good for them in the long term.

Too much nuts or nut butter

I have come across several articles on nuts and seeds, many of which recommend nuts and seeds as a very good paleo diet. Though probably most of our ancestors eat nuts and seeds, they are natural to some extent, yet nuts and seeds can still be irritating to the gut and most of them have a bad fatty acid profile. If you are struggling with your health or weight, I recommend limiting your consumption of most nuts and seeds and maybe even avoid them entirely until your health is under control and your digestion is perfect. If you remove them from your diet and add them back a little later on, you should be able to see if they affect you in a negative way or not and hence decide whether to permanently leave them out of your diet or take a little of nuts and seeds in your diet.

Not enough salt

It is an established fact that excess salt can be a problem, but also removing salt completely can certainly lead to issues as well. I have seen many people who started having issues with low blood pressure on a Paleo diet that have been resolved easily by adding a little natural sea salt here and there in their food. Some people try to imitate our ancestors too much and forget that our ancestors probably went out of their way to get a little extra sodium in their diet. There is a reason, after all, why salty is one of the main tastes we can discern. Hence, I recommend that you balance your salt intake because both the deficiency and excess have negative impact on our bodies. Do not take too little, as this will sabotage the eventual expected results of good health when on paleo diet.

Not enough carbs

What is generally observed is that a whole lot of people who embark on paleo diet become very carb phobic and associates carbohydrates with instant fat gain. We have to keep in mind that fat gain is much more complicated than that, and we are well adapted to function on carbs or fat for energy. For this reason, a lot of people limit their carbohydrate intake to very low amounts. Even when adequate amounts of fat are consumed to make up for the lesser amount of carbohydrates, and when we limit the amounts of carbs consumed too much, this can lead to intense cravings and indulging in unhealthy foods. Sources of starchy carbohydrates are especially feared because they are concentrated sources of carbs. If we start with the belief that carbohydrates are not bad per se, we can then see why it does not make sense to fear concentrated sources like starchy vegetables. Hence, make sure you do not become too cautious about carbohydrates and make sure you take sufficient quantity because your body needs it for energy and to avoid craving and indulging in foods that have been kicked out.

Note that carbohydrates in general should not be feared, carbohydrates from toxic sources like grains, legumes and refined sugar should.

Not enough fat

Again, in trying to imitate our Palaeolithic ancestors, some people still believe that in general, the quantity of fat consumed should be limited. Those people suggest that wild animals are very lean and that our ancestors did not consume much fat. However, it is often overlooked t that even very lean animals have plenty of fat tissues around their organs or between their skin and their muscles. Modern science also shows us that saturated fat is a great source of clean and non-toxic energy while too much lean protein can be a problem. Some people limit both fat and carbohydrate consumption, our two primary fuel sources, and either consume much more lean protein or consume less calories overall. For those who end up consuming too few calories, constant hunger is often felt and the energy levels usually plummet.

Eat good quantity of healthy natural saturated fat and those sources of non-toxic carbohydrates.

Not enough nutritious foods (nutrient deficiencies)

This problem is not seen very often, however, it is a possibility. In our modern world, eating a non-toxic diet is not enough, as many vitamins and minerals are needed to deal with all the stress and bad environmental factors that surround us. This simply means that chicken and vegetables day in and out is not going to deal with it. You should strive to frequently eat foods such as meat from grass-fed ruminants, fresh wild-caught fish, homemade stock, fermented vegetables, seafood, organs like liver and bone marrow, and a good variety of fresh vegetables.

Too much fruits

There is no need to say that fruits are certainly natural, however, most of them are loaded with fructose, which becomes toxic when consumed in high amounts. Just because many fruits are loaded with vitamin C, potassium, fiber and many natural anti-oxidant does not mean that the fructose in them is less toxic. A few pieces of fruit per day should not be any issue at all, but over-doing could be the reason why so many fail to lose the desired weight even on a Paleo diet.

Here is also yet another reason why starchy vegetables should be the carbohydrate source of choice. Starchy vegetables are converted to glucose only when digested so they are the healthier choice for most.

Forgetting about the other aspects of the lifestyle

While diet is the main focus and is certainly the central point of Paleo lifestyle, other lifestyle factors play a very important role on health and should not be forgotten. The three main other lifestyle factors to keep in mind other than diet are exercise, stress and sleep. Failure to have healthy habits in one or more of those other lifestyle factors can greatly limit or hinder your results. Bad sleep quality or lack of sleep can be especially harmful and no amount of healthy food is going to make up for it. Therefore, it is paramount to ensure the whole picture of the paleo diet is observed because only this will yield the desired health result.

Some other general reasons include the following:

Not fully committing ourselves to the paleo lifestyle

Doing the diet only to some extent is something that many people seem to be doing. Feedbacks gotten from followers is that they have not observed any difference since they switched to paleo lifestyle, but still, they also have not committed themselves all the way. There was this close ally of mine who decided to give the diet a shot. She took the challenge head-on and committed herself 100% (totally) from the beginning. This continues for a few weeks and then temptation got the better of her: she queried what will one bowl of pasta going to do? It is hard to believe, but she felt the repercussions of this for the whole of the following week. Fatigue, stomach aches, nausea, you name it. Nevertheless, it all makes sense, if you eliminate all of the unwanted toxins from your diet and flush your body clean, but then dabble with something toxic, bad reactions are to be expected.

Someone that cheats frequently has not even allowed his or her body to dispose of all toxins; thus, they have yet to achieve their optimal state. Therefore, for those of you still questioning how you are feeling on the diet, if the results are not at their best, it could well be because you are preventing that from happening by not committing to the diet changes. Cheating and eating less desirable foods can be perfectly fine when done on an infrequent basis, but I strongly recommend to people who first commit to the diet to do it fully for at least the first 30 days. This will give their body a chance to get rid of the bulk of the toxins and be nourished by the more nutritious foods of Paleo.

Paleo orthorexia

This reason happens to be the exact opposite of the above. We have all come across extremists in our life and we know what they are like; latching on to a thing and there is no other way, so do not even try to convince them otherwise. I do not want to believe that there is anything wrong with this. In fact, there was a time in my life when I was exactly like this. Having said that, it is a problem when the extremist is not well informed. It is one thing to follow something because you believe it is the right thing to do, but it is another thing when you do not know why it is the right thing. This happen possibly just because someone with a voice or the one you trust said so.

There are two things I would want you to keep in mind right from the moment you become a part of the paleo community; we are no longer cavemen, and we do not know for sure what our ancestors ate anyway. Society has evolved and we have to evolve too. Downloading this book was only a matter of the click of a button, I can get recipe ideas across to you, and in fact, I can keep you informed on everything I do through various social media outlets. What I am saying here is that with evolution, we have gained access to something that our ancestors did not have, like modern science for example. Probably hundreds of centuries ago, no one knew what butter was, neither was white potato consumed in most parts of the world, but today, we can prove that these things are not bad for us on a fundamental and structural level. Just because they were not consumed then does not necessarily mean we need to continue running from them now. If we fail to include these harmless consumables to our diets, our eating habits will become much more difficult to maintain over time, leading to the unavoidable collapse.

Another part of Paleo orthorexia I must mention, is that many that embark on this journey try to do things too perfectly. I still see people counting their calorie intake or trying to calculate the amount of each vitamin or mineral they consume. This amount of attention to details is often a recipe for failure because it comes from the wrong assumption that the amount of calories consumed should be consciously controlled. So, if you will be able to embark on the paleo journey successfully. It is important not to be an extremist because it is not possible to eat exactly like the cavemen, also, do not be too perfect about the details as this put you under much pressure that will make things more difficult for you.

Strong cravings

I have already got into this topic a bit in the previous heading when I discuss "Not fully committing," but without doubt, goes deeper than just nibbling on something you should not. A common struggle when making any diet change in one's life is to leave the old behind. This could happen for several reasons, but it is mostly because our bodies crave for the things we love but we cannot have anymore. Another reason is our minds convince our bodies that we need what we are missing, when in fact; your body is not even craving it at all. Whether it is for the first reason I mentioned above or the second, it is something difficult to get a handle on, especially when we are addicted to the things which we crave for.

It can sometimes seem hard to believe, but with bad food, things we consume are physically addictive. Two of the most common would have to be gluten-containing foods and sugar. Probably this explains to you why you were experiencing headaches during your transition period, or cases of extreme hunger. For quite a good number of people, it becomes so difficult to manage; they either drop the diet entirely, or end up slotting themselves into the "Not fully committing" category. I guess the next thing on your mind is how do one manage fighting the temptations? Well, when it comes to food, stopping cold turkey seems to be the easiest option in the long run. Just like jumping into cold water, it is much easier to jump right in than to get into the water gradually. The longer you keep on consuming foods that you are addicted to, the harder it will be to move away from them. You are also not doing your body any favor by continuing to ingest such toxic foods. If you are committed, it is a matter of time, it will pass and you will do just fine.

Pricey lifestyle

Sometimes I just can't help but to think how weird it is to ever consider putting a price on our health. In fact, when I began following a Paleo Diet, I had a small food budget and I feared that I would not be able to get the best quality of food for myself. However, even at that time, my health came first, so I had to make some compromises in other aspects of my life to ensure it stayed this way. In no way am I denying that it does not cost to lead a healthier lifestyle, but you must always know that the cost difference is so minimal compared to what it means for your future.

It might greatly interest you to know that there are various ways around the high costs associated with being Paleo, but you certainly will have to work a little harder to save here and there. One great way is to plant your own herb and vegetable garden during the growing season. If you do not have the ability to do so, consider joining a Farmer's Co-op. You should also consider following a set meal plan. This helps a lot, because when you plan all meals, you are just purchasing what you need and do not have to worry about over-spending on things that will go to waste. Try to be open to spending a bit more time in the kitchen preparing your meals. It always costs more when you purchase something pre-made, although this is not a luxury often available to the Paleo community anyways. Finally, get connected with a local butcher or farmer. I have a few of them and I am always lucky to get my hands on a great variety at very reasonable prices. If I am lucky and someone has excess of something, I buy it all up at a low price and stock up my freezer! I also have one butcher who has no use for some organ meats, as he does not have enough market for it, so he just throws it my way at no cost. Every point I stated above will help you save money even while you pursue the best for your health by going paleo but as I said, there is always more work involved when you want to cut corners and spend less. As for me, I would go extra miles to ensure I live an optimal healthy life, and in the case of being Paleo, I really do not think that extent is far from being attainable.

The convenience factor

People who are not fully committed struggle with the convenience factor.. As I have said on many occasions, following a Paleo Diet involves more time given to food and its preparation. Not just this, but for those who are concerned with the source of their meat, fruits and vegetables, there can be a great deal of work involved in setting up connections with local farmers and butchers. Once this is established, you may have to cope with traveling a short distance to collect your fresh produce and meats. Bringing all of these into consideration, I will ask: is it really enough to pull the plug on such a healthy alternative lifestyle? It sure is not for me! I quite enjoy the relationships I have made through various suppliers. Believe it or not, I have also built much greater bonds with people over food preparation. Sure, you cannot always prepare a huge meal in minimal time, but why not make the food a central part of your life. It is something that we all encounter on a frequent basis throughout our daily lives, so no matter how much someone likes the topic of food, at least you know that you can relate on some level about it. My aim here is to give you ways to turn something that seems inconvenient into something that is not that big of a burden after all.

Note that prevention is not the same as cure. People who have lived in the modern world, their whole lives might need more intensive intervention than people who have always been healthy.

NOTE THE FOLLOWING LESSONS

Pair Diet with Exercise

Paleo has a close connection with exercise. Moreover, while the "sport of fitness" is not for everyone, the idea that a diet and exercise plan should be part of a completely healthy lifestyle approach is always a good one: Research shows that emphasizing the two together is the best way to achieve weight loss. I would strongly encourage you to try walking out in addition to being on paleo diet and I can assure you that you will be glad you did because the results are enormous.

Achieve a Good Salt Balance

By getting rid of processed foods, which are the major source of sodium in the average diet, Paleo eaters eat a low-sodium diet without even trying. What is more, the plan provides nearly twice the typical amount of potassium than a typical average diet contains. That combination of low sodium and high potassium is a recipe for good vascular health and low blood pressure.

Choose Good Fats

The Paleo diet shuns hydrogenated vegetable oils in favor of single source fats like avocados, olive oil, flaxseed oil and coconut oil.

Cook For Yourself

Strict eating guidelines make restaurant dining and quick snacks at the vending machine a little trickier. This means that most of the food you eat comes from your own kitchen. In addition, it means you know exactly what is in it and how it will affect your body. Hence, put effort in to ensuring you personally cook what you eat.

Do not Count Calories

Paleolithic hunter-gatherers certainly did not count calories therefore, it is important you also do not count calories. While calories do count (you will gain weight if you eat a huge number of them), they are also not a metric of healthfulness. Nutritionists agree that calories are merely a jumping off point toward looking at the health value of food. Nutrient density is a far better measure for health.

Paleo Diet

CHAPTER FOUR

CLINICAL STUDIES OF PEOPLE THAT HAVE TURNED THEIR HEALTH AROUND USING THE PALEO DIET

"Clinical trials have shown that the Paleo Diet is the optimum diet that can lower the risk of cardiovascular disease, blood pressure, markers of inflammation, help with weight loss, reduce acne, promote optimum health and athletic performance," Loren Cordain, Ph.D., Colorado State University professor and author of The Paleo Diet told WebMD

1. Kelly

Having experienced his best performance after four weeks on The Paleo Diet, U.S. Olympic Triathlete coach Joe Friel used The Paleo Diet to coach national and international caliber athletes. However, this performance enhancing diet is not just for Olympic hopefuls. The Paleo Diet has helped others just like me to overcome personal challenges and poor health. I would like to share Kelly's story to encourage others to join her in turning their obstacles into triumphs. After an embarrassing failure to climb Mt. Hoffman, Kelly turned her life around to make it to the top of Yosemite's highest peak. With the help of Chris LaLanne (who continues granduncle Jack LaLanne's fitness legacy), she learned to use nutrition and exercise to regain lost fitness. Chris introduced Kelly to the benefits of The Paleo Diet, and here is what that has meant to Kelly:

"It was spring of 2008 when I finally had had enough: enough with being uncomfortable in my own skin, enough with being incredulous at the reflection in the mirror, enough with disparity between who I thought I was and my actual physical reality. I had always been athletic throughout school and in college (swim team, crew team) and on my own without the structure of the NCAA (adventure racing and marathons). Then a series of injuries and their subsequent surgeries and rehabs had me 'out of the game' for over three years. When a photo assignment came to shoot a portrait on top of Mt. Hoffman, Yosemite's highest peak, I took it with relish. 'That is right up my alley,' I thought. The panting, sweating difficulty I had on the climb (and inability to make it to the summit) was so embarrassing it was not just a wake-up call, it was a five alarm/bucket of cold water/shake you out of bed realization. This is what I had become-unfit, flabby and fat. I started going to my local gym using the treadmill and stair mill. I counted calories. I was never a 'junk food junkie,' but portion control was not part of my vernacular either. I thought a calorie was a calorie, regardless of the source. Of course, I did lose a few pounds as will happen on 1,000 - 1,500 calories a day, but I was ALWAYS hungry - stomach growling kind of hungry. I knew this was a battle and it needs reinforcements, and help arrived when I stepped through the doors of LaLanne Fitness. I did the 'Baseline' workout and although I am sure I was another panting, sweating mess, all I remember was that it was fun. Chris laid out the interconnectivity of the CrossFit model: strength/speed/flexibility/diet in the simplest common sense approach. The irony is that it is far from common. Fads and quick fixes are much more numerous despite being ineffective repeatedly. I saw results from the CrossFit workouts immediately. I had never lifted weights beyond bicep curls, and now I was giddy about strength workouts. I had to do almost everything scaled, but I did it. I had good fitness momentum but as soon as I addressed my diet, my health and capabilities went to the next level. First, I learned and incorporated the Zone Diet. I admit that I struggled at first because I was forced to pay attention to my food. No more mindless grabbing of the cereal box and having my third or fourth bowl of the day. Now I was enlightened to the fact that a calorie is not just a calorie. Fat is not bad and the USDA's food pyramid holy grail of grains is not always good...A leaner, fitter athlete kept emerging. I was having success but realized even with my Zone block approach, I was still eating some heavily processed foods. Food bars and soymilk were part of my daily intake. Chris LaLanne introduced us to The Paleo Diet at a Saturday nutrition talk. What a revelation. It took baby steps, but my 5+-years addiction to vanilla soymilk ended. In fact, my sweet tooth became manageable for the very first time - EVER. Now if I have a 'treat' (such a misnomer!), I feel the negative effects (sluggish, headache, sugar seeking) within the hour. I have no idea why I thought it was okay to not give my body good and clean fuel when I would never do that to my car. Strange. Chris has us keep nutrition logs so there was accountability amongst my fellow CrossFitters, but more importantly to myself. It has been one year since this journey began. My 60 + pound weight loss accounts for all the new clothes in the closet, and The Paleo Diet accounts for the complete organic makeover of my cupboards and refrigerator. My foods are now perishable instead of shelf stable. And, I'm 'back in the game' going for the summit every day."

2. Paleolithic Diet Clinical Trials conducted in Sweden

A group of people with health issues was placed on paleo diet for three months and the following were administered according to paleo diet regulations:

- Reduced their caloric intake from 2,478 to 1,584 kcal

- Increased their percentage protein and fat, while decreasing carbohydrate

- Reduced saturated fat, increased dietary cholesterol, decreased sodium intake, increased potassium

The following were observed:

- Lost 2.3 kg (5 lb)

- Decreased waist circumference, blood pressure and PAI-1

- Greater fat loss in the midsection and a trend toward greater weight loss

- A remarkable improvement in glucose tolerance

- A decrease in fasting glucose

- Fasting insulin plummeted by 68%. HOMA-IR, a measure of insulin resistance, decreased by 72%

- This study adds to the evidence that no matter what your gender or genetic background, a diet roughly consistent with our evolutionary past can bring major health benefits

3. Details: 10 healthy women with a BMI over 27 consumed a modified Paleolithic diet for 5 weeks.

Main outcomes measured were liver fat, muscle cell fat and insulin sensitivity.

Weight Loss: The women lost an average of 4.5 kg (9.9 lbs.) and had an 8 cm (3.1 inches) reduction in waist circumference.

Liver and Muscle Fat: The fat content of liver and muscle cells are a risk factor for metabolic disease. In this study, the women had an average reduction in liver fat of 49%, but no significant effect on the fat content of muscle cells.

Other Health Effects:

- Blood pressure went down from an average of 125/82 mmHg to 115/75 mmHg, although it was only statistically significant for diastolic blood pressure (the lower number).

- Fasting blood sugars reduced by 6.35 mg/dL (0.35 mmol/L) and fasting insulin levels reduced by 19%.

- Total cholesterol reduced by 33 mg/dL (0.85 mmol/L).

- Triglycerides went down by 35 mg/dL (0.39 mmol/L).

- LDL cholesterol went down by 25 mg/dL (0.65 mmol/L).

- HDL cholesterol reduced by 7 mg/dL (0.18 mmol/L).

- ApoB reduced by 129 mg/L (14.3%).

Conclusion: During the 5-weeks trial, the women lost weight and had major reductions in liver fat. They also had improvements in several important health markers.

Paleo Diet

CHAPTER FIVE

WHAT PROFESSIONALS AND DOCTORS SAY ABOUT PALEO DIET

Loren Cordain, PhD, Colorado State University professor and author of *The PaleoDiet*.

The Paleo diet is a very healthy diet. Clinical trials have shown that the Paleo Diet is the optimum diet that can lower the risk of cardiovascular disease, blood pressure, markers of inflammation, help with weight loss, reduce acne and promote optimum health and athletic performance. Even though grains and dairy seem healthful, Cordain says our "genome has not really adapted to these foods, which can cause inflammation at the cellular level and promote disease." Eating like our ancestors 80% of the time offers health benefits. He suggests trying the diet for two weeks to see if you feel better on the plan.

Kathleen Zelman, MPH, RD, is director of nutrition for WebMD

A diet that includes whole, unprocessed foods is the basis of most all healthy diet recommendations. However, so are whole grains, low-fat dairy, and legumes. If the Paleo or Caveman diet appeals to you, be sure to supplement the plan with Calcium and Vitamin D. Eliminating all grains, dairy, processed foods, sugar, and more will most likely lead to weight loss. But it may be tough to follow this plan long-term due to the diet's strict nature. Paleo diet is helpful in overcoming several diseases.

Jeff Novick MS, RD Dietitian & Nutritionist

Many of the changes the Paleo diet recommends are healthy and have strong evidence behind them. The focus of the Paleo diet on removing processed and refined foods is excellent and should be heeded. However, the recommendation to eliminate intact whole grains, legumes and unrefined unprocessed starchy vegetables is misguided. The diet does fall short of meeting the daily-recommended intakes for certain micronutrients. A 9.3% increase in income is needed to consume a Paleolithic diet that meets all daily-recommended intakes except for calcium.

New research on the diet of Australopithecus Sediba

According to the research, "Almost two million years after their last meals, two members of a pre human species in southern Africa left traces in their teeth of what they had eaten then, as well as over a lifetime of foraging. Scientists were surprised to find that these hominines apparently lived almost exclusively on a diet of leaves, fruits, wood and bark." Benjamin H. Passey, a geochemist at Johns Hopkins University says "Paleo diet" advocates are way off track if they still think that grains, i.e. seeds of grasses, are only a recent addition to the diet of humans. He adds, "One thing people probably don't realize is that humans are basically grass eaters. We eat grass in the form of the grains we use to make breads, noodles, cereals and beers, and we eat animals that eat grass. It seems Human evolution might look something like this: the grass-eaters went extinct, but the grass-*seed* eaters thrived.

Jow Friel - U.S. Olympic triathlon coach. Friel and Loren Cordain, PhD, authored the authoritative book on the subject, *The Paleo Diet for Athletes*, which outlines a couple of changes athletes should make to the basic Paleo diet.

Most importantly, a Paleo diet – as opposed to a high-starch and sugar diet, like many athletes eat – can have the following effects: more vitamins and antioxidants to keep a strong immune system; increased fat oxidation, which helps long-event endurance; balanced pH levels; and better retained and recovered muscles.

All of which makes you faster in the long run.

European Journal of Clinical Nutrition

Even short-term consumption of a paleolithic type diet improves BP and glucose tolerance, decreases insulin secretion, increases insulin sensitivity and improves lipid profiles without weight loss in healthy sedentary humans.

Researchers at the University of California at San Francisco

According to these researchers, those who ate like cavemen saw significant drops in blood pressure, cholesterol, triglycerides, as well as blood sugar.

Lindeberg S, et al. A Paleolithic diet improves glucose tolerance more than a Mediterranean-like diet in individuals with ischaemic heart disease. Diabetologia, 2007. Diabetologia, 2007.

Details: 29 men with heart disease and elevated blood sugars or type 2 diabetes, were randomized to either a Paleolithic diet (n=14) or a Mediterranean-like diet (n=15). Neither group was calorie restricted.

The major outcomes measured were glucose tolerance, insulin levels, weight and waist circumference. This study went on for 12 weeks.

Glucose Tolerance: The glucose tolerance test measures how quickly glucose is cleared from the blood. It is a marker for insulin resistance and diabetes.

Weight Loss: Both groups lost a significant amount of weight, 5 kg (11 lbs.) in the paleo group and 3.8 kg (8.4 lbs.) in the control group. However, the difference was not statistically significant between groups.

The paleo diet group had a 5.6cm (2.2inches) reduction in waist circumference, compared to 2.9cm (1.1inches) in the control group. The difference was statistically significant.

A few important points:

The 2-hour Area Under the Curve (AUC) for blood glucose went down by 36% in the paleo group, compared to 7% in the control group.

Every patient in the paleo group ended up having normal blood sugars, compared to 7 of 15 patients in the control group.

The paleo group ended up eating 451 fewer calories per day (1344 compared to 1795) without intentionally restricting calories or portions.

Conclusion: A Paleolithic diet lead to greater improvements in waist circumference and glycemic control, compared to a Mediterranean-like diet.

Osterdahl M, et al. Effects of a short-term intervention with a Paleolithic diet in healthy volunteers European Journal of Clinical Nutrition, 2008.

Details: 14 healthy medical students (5 male, 9 female) were instructed to eat a Paleolithic diet for 3 weeks. There was no control group.

Weight Loss: Weight decreased by 2.3kg (5 lbs.), body mass index decreased by 0.8 and waist circumference went down by 1.5cm (0.6inches).

Other Markers: Systolic blood pressure went down by 3mmHg.

Conclusion: The individuals lost weight and had a mild reduction in waist circumference and systolic blood pressure.

Jonsson T, et al. Beneficial effects of a Paleolithic diet on cardiovascular risk factors in type 2 diabetes: a randomized crossover pilot study. Cardiovascular Diabetology, 2009.

Details: 13 individuals with type 2 diabetes were placed on either a Paleolithic diet or a typical Diabetes diet in a crossover study. They were on each diet for 3 months at a time.

Weight Loss: On the paleo diet, the participants lost 3kg (6.6 lbs.) more weight and lost 4cm (1.6inches) off their waistlines, compared to the Diabetes diet.

Other Markers:

- HbA1c (a marker for 3-month blood sugar levels) decreased by 0.4% more on the paleo diet.

- HDL increased by 3mg/dL (0.08mmol/L) on the paleo diet compared to the Diabetes diet.

- Triglycerides went down by 35mg/dL (0.4mmol/L) on the paleo diet compared to the Diabetes diet.

Frassetto, et al. Metabolic and physiologic improvements from consuming a Paleolithic, hunter-gatherer type diet European Journal of Clinical Nutrition, 2009.

Details: 9 healthy individuals consumed a Paleolithic diet for 10 days. Their calories intake were controlled to ensure that they would not lose weight. There was no control group.

Health Effects:

Total Cholesterol went down by 16%.

LDL Cholesterol went down by 22%.

Triglycerides went down by 35%.

Insulin AUC went down by 39%.

Diastolic Blood Pressure went down by 3.4 mmHg.

BULLETPROOF LINKED PALEO DIET WITH CANCER, GOING AS FAR AS SAYING HIGH CARB DIET CONTRIBUTED TO STEVE JOB'S DEATH.

The following are his views:

According to him, Mr. Jobs trusted his health to the Dean Ornish, high-carb, low fat, macrobiotic, pseudo-vegan diet. He used the result gotten by some German researchers from the University Hospital of Würzburg on the benefits of low carbs diets for cancer patients to buttress his views.

The German researchers said that over the last few years, evidence has accumulated suggesting that by systematically reducing the amount of dietary carbohydrates (CHO), one could *suppress or* at least delay the emergence of cancer, and that proliferation of already existing *tumor* cells could be slowed down.

By limiting carbohydrates, you can decrease your risk of cancer and improve your chances of recovery. Also, it could slow down the progress of an existing cancer.

The researchers went even further to suggest a low-carb diet could be preventative against cancer. So much for "no statistical evidence a vegan (ahem, high-carb) diet contributes to cancer."

According to this review, a high-carb diet is believed to contribute to cancer in six ways:

1. Cancer cells depend almost exclusively on glucose. The mitochondria of cancer cells are dysfunctioning (because of UCP2), which prevents them from metabolizing ketone bodies or free fatty acids. Chronically elevated glucose levels feed tumors and cancer cells. Elevated insulin levels also promote the growth of tumors.

"Evidence exists that chronically elevated blood glucose, insulin and IGF1 levels facilitate tumorigenesis and worsen the outcome in cancer patients." The best way to fix this problem is to lower both glucose and insulin levels. This method is especially effective in people with advanced stage cancer (like Steve Jobs'). "High fat, low CHO diets aim at accounting for these metabolic alterations. Studies conducted so far have shown that such diets are safe and likely beneficial, in particular for advanced stage cancer patients."

2. High insulin and insulin like growth factor, "resulting from chronic ingestion of CHO-rich Western diet meals," can "directly promote tumor cell proliferation via the insulin/IGF-1 signaling pathway." High insulin levels from a high-carb diet promote tumor growth.

3. Many cancer patients develop insulin resistance, which can make a high-carb diet deleterious to their health in numerous ways. As the researchers stated, patients may "profit from an increased protein and fat intake."

4. High amounts of circulating glucose are extremely inflammatory. Inflammation exacerbates almost all diseases, including cancer.

5. Rodent studies have found ketone bodies to inhibit cancer cell growth. This has yet to be proven in humans – but the clinical observations are very strong.

6. A grain-based diet contributes to inflammation, depletes nutrient stores, and prevents the absorption of nutrients.

Caloric restriction is another effective way to lower both insulin and glucose levels, but it comes with some negative side effects. Cancer patients often lose weight and become malnourished during their treatment, and starving them isn't going to improve the situation. Luckily, carbohydrate restriction can take advantage of almost all the benefits of caloric deprivation, without starving the patient.

"CHO restriction mimics the metabolic state of calorie restriction or – in the case of KDs (ketogenic diets) – fasting. The beneficial effects of calorie restriction and fasting on cancer risk and progression are well established. CHO restriction thus opens the possibility to target the same underlying mechanisms without the side-effects of hunger and weight loss."

By cutting carbs (and adding MCT oil to enter ketosis faster), cancer patients might be able to utilize the benefits of caloric restriction, without cutting calories and suffering from malnourishment. Speaking of malnourishment...

The most interesting part of this study was the role grains played in causing cancer. Vegans, vegetarians, and most Americans get the majority of their carbs from grains. As the researchers pointed out, grain based carbs might be the main problem, not carbs in general.

A high-carb diet is bad for cancer patients, but a grain-based diet is even worse.

"Usually, CHO restriction is not only limited to avoiding sugar and other high-GI foods, but also to a reduced intake of grains. Grains can induce inflammation in susceptible individuals due to their content of omega-6 fatty acids, lectins and gluten [159, 160]. In particular gluten might play a key role in the pathogenesis of auto-immune and inflammatory disorders and some malignant diseases."

There are hundreds of reasons grains contribute to cancer, so this article will cover just a few.

Grains cause inflammation by themselves, regardless of whether the diet is low in carbohydrates or not. This occurs through several pathways.

Grains contain omega-6 fats, lectins, phytates, damaging fiber, and gluten. Anything that contributes to inflammation will make cancer worse, but gluten has several special characteristics that exacerbate cancer growth. Gluten overstimulates the release of zonulin, a protein that regulates the space between epithelial cells in the small intestine. This causes dysregulation between cells that promotes cancer growth throughout the digestive tract.

In the small intestine, gluten triggers the release of zonulin, a protein that regulates the tight junctions between epithelial cells and therefore intestinal, but also blood-brain barrier function. Recent evidence suggests that overstimulation of zonulin in susceptible individuals could dysregulate intercellular communication promoting tumorigenesis at specific organ sites"

Reducing total carbohydrate load was not nearly as important as removing grain based carbohydrates. It is sad to think that Steve Jobs was being told to eat not only a high-carb diet, but also to eat 8-11 servings of "healthy" whole grains a day.

The study authors were quick to offer a solution: the paleo diet. Both animal and human beings have shown the paleo diet is extremely effective at improving glucose tolerance and decreasing your risk for disease – far more so than the grain based Mediterranean diet. Switching to a paleo diet would remove grains, and lower the total glycemic index of the person's diet. Vegetables have a far lower glycemic index than grains. Studies have shown this result in better glucose control and less inflammation.

"Paleolithic-type diets, by definition exclude grain products, have been shown to improve glycemic control and cardiovascular risk factors more effectively than typically recommended low-fat diets rich in whole grains.

These diets are not necessarily very low CHO diets, but focus on replacing high-GI modern foods with fruits and vegetables, in this way reducing the total GL."

Humans are not made to eat a grain-based diet. Our genes are made to respond to certain foods both positively and negatively. Cancer is a negative response.

The researchers were smart to mention that diet is not the only factor in the development of cancer. There are other components such as "regular physical activity, sun exposure, sufficient sleep, low chronic stress and the lack of foods that would also not have been available to our pre-neolithic ancestors." Okay, so diet was still the most important part.

NOTE THE FOLLOWING

▶A Paleo diet should be high in fat, moderate in animal protein and low to be moderate in carbohydrate. Calorie counting is not encouraged, neither is portion control. Eat generous amounts of saturated fats like coconut oil and butter or clarified butter. Good amounts of animal protein, which includes red meat, poultry, pork, eggs, organs (liver, kidney, heart...), wild caught fish and shellfish. Do not be scared of eating the fatty cuts and meals with proteins, which contain fat as well. Learn to cook with bones in the form of stocks and broths.

►Eat generous amounts of fresh or frozen vegetables, either cooked or raw and served with fat. Starchy vegetables like sweet potatoes and yams are also great as a source of non-toxic carbohydrates.

►Eat low to moderate amounts of fruits and nuts. Try to eat mostly fruits low in sugar and high in antioxidants like berries as well as nuts high in omega-3, low in omega-6 and low in total polyunsaturated fat like macadamia nuts. If you have an autoimmune disease, digestive problems or trying to lose weight faster, consider cutting off fruits and nuts altogether.

►It is better to choose pasture raised and grass fed meat from local, environmentally conscious farms. If not possible, choose lean cuts of meat and supplement your fat with coconut oil, butter or clarified butter. Also preferably, choose organic, local and/or seasonal fruits and vegetables.

►Cut out all cereal grains and legumes from your diet. This includes, but not limited to wheat, rye, barley, oats, corn, brown rice, soy, peanuts, kidney beans, pinto beans, navy beans and black-eyed peas.

▶Cut out all vegetables, hydrogenated and partly hydrogenated oils. This includes, but not limited to margarine, soybean oil, corn oil, peanut oil, canola oil, safflower oil and sunflower oil. Olive oil and avocado oil are fine, but do not cook with them, use them in salad dressings and to drizzle over food.

▶Get rid of added sugar, soft drinks, all packaged sweets and juices (including fruit juices). As a rule of thumb, if it is in a box, do not eat it. At the grocery store, visit primarily the meat, fish and produce sections.

▶Remove dairy products other than butter and maybe heavy cream. You do not need dairy, but if you cannot live without it, I is advisable you consider raw, full fat and/or fermented dairy.

▶Eat when you are hungry and do not stress if you skip a meal or even two. You do not have to eat three square meals a day, do what feels most natural.

▶ As much as possible, eliminate external stressors in your life and sleep at least eight hours per night. Try to wake up without an alarm and go to bed when it gets dark.

▶Do not over exercise, keep your training sessions short and intense and do them only a few times per week. Take some extra time off if you feel tired. Consider short and intense sprinting sessions instead of very long cardio sessions.

▶Consider supplementing with vitamin D and probiotics. Levels of magnesium, iodine and vitamin K2 should also be optimized. In addition, iodine can be obtained from seaweeds. It is most likely that you do not need multivitamin or other supplements.

▶Another thing that you must try to do is always try to play in the sun, have fun, laugh, smile, relax, discover, travel, learn and enjoy life like a daring adventure.

▶Epidemiological studies show that diets rich in Monounsaturated and Omega-3 fats dramatically reduce the instances of obesity, cancer, diabetes, heart disease and cognitive decline.

Paleo dieters hence eat the following

• Meat, especially birds, wild caught fish and grass fed ruminants. Variation exists among paleo belief as to how fatty Paleolithic meats would have been. Hunter-gatherers living in coastal areas would likely have eaten reasonable amounts of fat from marine mammals they hunted as the Inuit do today. Others would have eaten less animal fat.

• The offal of the animals listed above.

• Large amounts of vegetables.

• Fruits (limited by some).

• Tubers, such as sweet potatoes and sometimes white potatoes (limited by some).

• Butter, lard, tallow, coconut oil, and other fats and oils not made from grains or seeds.

• Fermented foods such as sauerkraut, kombucha, and kefir.

• No added sugar, especially high fructose corn syrup.

• No grains or legumes, though some argue that soaking and/or fermenting them makes them acceptable.

Dairy is often excluded or limited, but high fat or fermented dairy is often included by so-called 'lacto-paleos' or 'Primal'

PALEO DIET:
SNACKS

Paleo Sweet and Spicy Potato Chips

About 20 minutes to prepare

Ingredients

Two large sweet potatoes

One teaspoon of chili powder

Sea salt

Half cup of olive oil

Preparation

Peel and slice the potatoes on a mandolin slicer as thin as you can get them. Line a sheet pan with paper towels.

Pour about 1/2 inch of olive oil in a deep skillet. Turn the heat on medium high and allow the oil to heat up for several minutes. Add one of the chips to the oil; if it sizzles, it's ready.

Cook the potatoes in an even layer, in batches, until all are cooked. Season with chili powder and sea salt to taste and serve immediately.

Makes 6 servings

Baked Carrot Fries

Takes about 30 minutes to prepare

Ingredients

Six carrots

Two tablespoon of olive oil

One pinch of salt

A quarter teaspoon of sumac

One sprig of mint (finely chopped)

Preparation

Preheat oven to 425^0F

Cut off ends of carrots, slice length wise, and slice each side into 3 pieces.

Mix carrot fries in the mixture of olive oil, sumac and salt until they are evenly coated.

Place fries on a parchment lined cookie sheet and cook fries for 10 minutes. Remove fries from oven and turn them. Increase heat to 450 and cook for additional 10 minutes.

Let it cool for 10 minutes. Sprinkle mint on top of carrot fries.

Makes 4 servings

Baked Apples

Takes about 20 minutes to prepare

Ingredients

Two apples (cored and quartered)

One tablespoon of Ghee

One tablespoon of ground cinnamon

Preparation

Preheat oven to 350^0F.

Place the cored and quartered apples in an aluminum foil pouch. Drizzle with cinnamon and add the ghee. Close pouch tightly.

Cook in oven for about 15 minutes.

Open pouch gently and serve.

Makes 2 servings

Kale Chips

Takes about 40 minutes to prepare

Ingredients

One bunch of kale

Olive oil

Sea salt

Preparation

Wash kale very well and dry it.

Preheat oven to 350^{0}F. Use parchment paper to line the inside of a rimmed baking sheet.

Cut the middle stem off and cut remaining leaves to desired size.

Place the kale in a single layer on the baking sheet; make sure leaves don't make contact.

Spray both sides of the kale with oil and season with salt.

Place kale in oven for about 12 minutes, flip all kales and cook for about 5 minutes until crispy (not brown). Serve.

Paleo Fried Plantains

Takes about 10 minutes to prepare

Ingredients

Two ripe plantains

One tablespoon ghee or coconut oil.

One teaspoon of ground cinnamon

Half teaspoon of sea salt

Preparation

Peel plantains and cut them diagonally (1-11/2 inches)

Add coconut oil to a nonstick skillet over medium heat (entire surface of skillet should be coated)

Put in plantains and cook each side for 2-3 minutes.

Put in a serving plate, dust with cinnamon and sprinkle with sea salt.

Makes 3 servings

Paleo Chili Lime Broiled Avocado

Takes about ten minutes to prepare

Ingredients

One avocado (pitted)

One lime (juiced)

Half teaspoon of chili powder

One teaspoon of honey

Sea salt

Preparation

Preheat broiler to high heat. Drizzle avocado halves with lime juice and honey.

Lay on baking sheet cut size up. Broil for about 5 minutes until the flesh of the avocado begins to blister. Take out of oven and sprinkle with chili powder and salt. Serve it warm.

Makes 2 servings

Creamy Pesto Cashew Dip

Takes about 4-6 hours to prepare

Ingredients

Two cups of raw cashew

A quarter cup of olive oil

Half teaspoon of sea salt

One bunch of fresh basil leaves

One clove of garlic

A quarter teaspoon of black pepper

One lemon (juiced)

Sliced veggies

Preparation

Cover cashews with cold water in a large bowl. Leave it soaked for 4-6 hours and then drain. Rinse and drain again.

Blend the basil, garlic, and lemon juice. Then add the cashews and blend until creamy.

Gently sprinkle in the olive oil and continue processing until creamy.

Season with pepper and salt, then serve with sliced veggies.

Makes 8 servings

Paleo Homemade Applesauce

Takes about 45 minutes to prepare

Ingredients

Three pounds of Apples (peel, core and chop)

Half cup of either water or apple cider

One lemon (juiced)

Two to three tablespoon of honey

Half teaspoon of cinnamon

Preparation

Put all ingredients in a big pot. Boil and then reduce heat to a simmer.

Simmer for 20-30 minutes until apples are well broken down.

If you want it chunkier, serve as it is. Blend in a blender if you prefer it smoother. Store in a fridge.

Makes 6 servings

PALEO DIET:
SIDE DISHES

Paleo Garlic Mashed Cauliflower

Takes about 30 minutes to prepare

Ingredients

One head of Cauliflower (cut into florets)

Two cloves of garlic

Two tablespoon of olive oil

A quarter cup of coconut milk

Fresh chopped herbs (dill, rosemary, etc. this is optional)

Sea salt and fresh ground pepper

Preparation

Steam the cauliflower and garlic cloves in a steamer basket until it becomes very soft.

Transfer the above to a food processor and process until smooth. Instead of a processor, you can use a potato masher.

Stir in the coconut milk, olive oil, herbs (if you want) and season with salt and pepper before serving.

Makes 4 servings

Crispy Vegetable Cakes

Takes about 30 minutes to prepare

Ingredients

A quarter cup of almond flour

One tablespoon of parsley (freshly chopped)

One cup of baby spinach (finely chopped)

One teaspoon of thyme

Two tablespoons of olive oil

One parsnip (peeled and grated)

One carrot (peeled and grated)

One garlic clove (minced)

One onion (diced)

One red bell pepper (finely chopped)

One egg

Sea salt and fresh ground pepper

Preparation

Add all of the vegetables in a bowl with the herbs, egg and almond flour. Season with pepper and salt, then mix well. Form into 4 patties

Heat the oil in a skillet on medium-high. Adjust temperature as needed. Add the vegetable cakes and cook until golden brown on both sides. Serve right away.

Makes 4 servings

Roasted Butternut Squash with Crispy Sage Leaves

Takes about one hour in total.

Ingredients

One butternut squash (peeled and cubed)

Three tablespoons of oil

Twelve sage leaves

Sea salt and fresh ground pepper

Preparation

Preheat oven to 400^0F.

Mix the squash with two tablespoons of oil and a pinch of pepper and salt.

Lay this on a baking sheet in a single layer and roast for about 20 minutes.

Take it out of the oven, stir and continue roasting for 10-15 minutes until the squash is tender and brown.

Before you serve it, heat remaining oil in a skillet. Add sage leaves and cook for about one minute until just crisp, then mix with the squash.

Makes 4 servings

Zucchini Fritters

Takes about 20 minutes

Ingredients

Two zucchini (grated)

One teaspoon of sea salt

Two tablespoons of coconut flour

Four scallions (sliced)

One egg

Two tablespoons of coconut oil

One teaspoon of black pepper

One teaspoon of cayenne pepper

Preparation

Mix the shredded zucchini and sea salt in a bowl and leave for about 10 minutes. Then squeeze water out of the zucchini and transfer to another bowl.

Stir in the coconut flour, egg, scallions, cayenne and pepper. Pour the coconut oil into a medium skillet over medium high heat. Once melted, form six fritters and place them in the skillet. Brown on each side, then place on a paper-towel lined plate and serve immediately. If you like, garnish it with more scallions.

Makes 6 servings

Sauteed Kale

Preparation takes about 15 minutes.

Ingredients

Four cups of kale (chopped)

One small onion (diced)

Two garlic cloves (minced)

One tablespoon of olive oil

One tablespoon of red wine vinegar

Two tablespoons of almonds (sliced)

Salt to taste

Preparation

Heat olive oil in a skillet over medium heat. Add the onions and sauté for about five minutes.

Add garlic, kale, almonds, and red wine vinegar.

Cook for about 7 minutes until kale is soft.

Season with salt and serve

Makes about 2 servings

Crispy Cauliflower Cakes

Takes about 30 minutes to cook

Ingredients

One head of cauliflower

Two teaspoon of garlic powder

One tablespoon of coconut oil (melted)

Three tablespoons of coconut flour

Two tablespoons of chives (chopped)

Two eggs

One teaspoon of salt

3-4 tablespoons of coconut oil.

Preparation

Cut the cauliflower into florets. Pulse the florets in a food processor until they become a rice like texture. Move the riced cauliflower to a large microwave-safe mixing bowl and microwave on high for 2-3 minutes until cooked through. Remove the bowl from the microwave and set aside to cool for about 5 minutes.

Add the melted coconut oil, chopped chives, coconut flour, garlic powder, eggs, and salt to the mixing bowl. Mix until all ingredients are well combined.

Use your hands to form the mixture into 6-8 patties. Set aside.

Heat the coconut oil in a skillet over medium heat. Fry the patties in the coconut oil until browned, about 2-3 minutes per side. Remove the patties from the oil and place on a paper towel lined plate to remove any excess oil. Serve.

Makes 6 servings

Honey Ginger Carrots

Ingredients

One pound of carrots

A quarter cup of olive oil

A quarter cup of honey

A quarter teaspoon of sea salt

One tablespoon of sesame seeds

Three tablespoons of coconut aminos

One inch of fresh ginger

Preparation

Preheat oven to 400^0F

Peel carrots, cut them in half lengthwise. Place them in a baking dish and set aside.

Mix together olive oil, sea salt, honey, fresh ginger and coconut aminos in a bowl, then pour the mixture over the carrots evenly.

Bake in oven for 35-40 minutes until tender.

Sprinkle with sesame seeds and serve.

Makes 4 servings

Sweet Potato Bites & Spicy Cilantro Aioli

Ingredients

Three- 3" sweet potatoes (cut into 1cubes)

One teaspoon of paprika

Salt and pepper

Two tablespoon of coconut oil

One egg

Half cup extra light virgin olive oil

Half cup Cilantro (finely chopped)

Juice from 1 lime (about 1 tablespoon)

Half Fresh jalapeño (diced, seeds and veins removed)

Preparation

Preheat oven to 400^0

Grease a large baking sheet with a tablespoon of coconut oil and spread out diced sweet potatoes uniformly. Sprinkle liberally with paprika, sea salt, and pepper. Mix the sweet potatoes for uniform coating with spices. Drizzle sweet potatoes with remaining tablespoon of coconut oil and add more spices if you wish. Cook for 15 minutes, mixing half way. While the sweet potatoes are cooking, start to prepare the Spicy Cilantro Aioli. Crack egg into a large mouthed mason jar. Add lime juice, salt and pepper, cilantro, chopped jalapeño, and 1/2 c olive oil. Blend all ingredients with submersion blender until creamy. Set aside.

Once potatoes are complete, serve as an appetizer on a nice plate with toothpicks and a side of the spicy cilantro aioli.

Makes 2 serving.

Curry Cauliflower Rice

Ingredients

One head Cauliflower

One tablespoon of olive oil

A quarter teaspoon of curry powder

A quarter teaspoon of turmeric

One-eighth of a teaspoon of ginger ground

Salt

Fresh parsley chopped, to garnish

Preparation

Cut cauliflower into florets with little stem. Place in food processor and pulse until it becomes a rice consistency.

Heat olive oil in skillet over medium heat and sauté cauliflower in it for about 5 minutes until soft.

Mix spices together in a bowl as cauliflower cooks. Stir into cauliflower ensuring uniform coating. Cook for about 3 minutes until fragrant. Season with salt and remove from heat.

Garnish with fresh parsley and serve.

Makes 2 servings

Bacon Jalapeno Mashed Sweet Potatoes

Ingredients

Four sweet potatoes

Two jalapenos (diced)

Four strips of cooked bacon diced

Half cup of coconut cream

Sea salt and black pepper

Preparation

Preheat oven to 400°F

Wash and pierce sweet potatoes with a fork and place on a baking sheet and put in oven. Cook for about 45 minutes.

Take out of oven let potatoes cool. Once cool enough, cut them in half and scoop the inside in to a bowl.

Stir in coconut cream and diced jalapenos. If you want creamier potatoes, use blender or hand mixer.

Fold in half the bacon. Season with sea salt and black pepper.

Divide mixture onto hallowed out sweet potatoes.

Transfer potatoes to a serving plate and garnish the top with bacon.

Serve immediately.

Makes 4 servings

Zucchini Noodles (easy)

Takes about 20 minutes to prepare

Ingredients

Two Zucchini (medium size)

One tablespoon of olive oil

One teaspoon of kosher salt

Preparation

Cut zucchini into noodles with a julienne peeler or spiral slicer. Sprinkle with salt on a paper towel and leave for about 10 minutes.

Squeeze the liquid from the noodles. Add the oil to a skillet over medium heat. Once warm, add noodles. Cook for about 5 minutes or desired tenderness.

Makes 4 servings

Buffalo Mushroom Skewers

Takes about 20 minutes to prepare

Ingredients

One pound of button mushrooms

Two tablespoons of olive oil

Half cup of hot sauce

Half teaspoon of sea salt

Preparation

Preheat oven to 375^{0}F

Clean mushroom carefully with damp paper towel making sure they don't get wet. Don't break or split the mushrooms, but can remove the stems if desired.

Mix the olive oil, hot sauce and salt in a bowl. Add mushrooms and toss to coat.

To cook mushrooms: thread them on skewers and set them on a baking sheet.

Makes 5 servings

Paleo Cauliflower Tabouli

Takes about 20 minutes to prepare

Ingredients

One clove of garlic

Half head of cauliflower

One small bunch of parsley (chop finely)

One lemon (juiced)

One tablespoon of finely chopped mint

One large tomato (diced)

Two tablespoon of olive oil

Sea salt and fresh ground pepper

Preparation

Put the cauliflower and the garlic in a food processor. Chop until the cauliflower is finely chopped.

Transfer it into a bowl and add the remaining ingredients. Mix until well combined. Chill until ready to serve.

Makes 4 servings

Paleo Sweet Potato Casserole

Takes about 45 minutes to prepare

Ingredients

6 not so big sweet potatoes (peel and cube)

Two tablespoon of orange juice

Half cup of coconut milk

Two tablespoon of coconut milk

One teaspoon of ginger

One teaspoon of cinnamon

Salt (pinch)

Topping

Two tablespoon of maple syrup

One cup of pecans (raw)

One teaspoon of cinnamon

One tablespoon of coconut oil

Half teaspoon of sea salt

Preparation

Preheat oven to 350°F. Place potatoes in a large pot and cover with cold water. Boil, reduce to simmer and cook for about 10 minutes until soft. Drain.

Transfer potatoes to a large bowl and mash well with a potato masher. Add the coconut milk, coconut oil, orange juice, ginger, cinnamon, and salt. Mix well, and spread into a casserole dish. Combine the ingredients for the topping in a bowl until pecans are well coated. Spread them over the potatoes and bake for 15 minutes.

Makes 8 servings

Green Bean Casserole

Takes about 45 minutes to prepare

Ingredients

Two pounds of fresh green beans (trimmed)

Two tablespoons of olive oil

One teaspoon of balsamic vinegar

Two cups of mushrooms (sliced)

Half cup of coconut milk

One onion (thinly sliced)

Half cup of almonds (sliced)

Sea salt and fresh ground pepper

Preparation

Preheat oven to 375^0 F.

Bring a large pot of salted water to a boil and prepare a large bowl of ice water. Add the green beans and cook for 5 minutes.

Drain and immediately plunge into the ice water. Let sit while you prepare the onions.

Heat a large skillet over medium heat and add the olive oil. Add the onions and mushrooms to the skillet and cook until well browned and caramelized. Add the vinegar, stir, and remove from heat.

Drain the beans and transfer to a casserole dish. Drizzle with coconut milk and top with the mushrooms and onions. Bake for 30 minutes. Remove from oven and sprinkle with the almonds before serving.

Curried Vegetable Skillet with Fried Eggs

Takes about 20 minutes to prepare

Ingredients

Four tablespoon of olive oil

One tablespoon of curry powder

Two leeks (sliced)

One carrot (grated)

Two cups of baby spinach

Two garlic cloves (minced)

Four eggs

Sea salt and fresh ground pepper

Preparation

To prepare leeks, cut off dark green parts and end. Slice stalk lengthwise, then slice. Submerge in large bowl of water to let all the dirt fall to bottom, about 5 minutes. Drain. A spinning colander works great for leeks!

Heat two tablespoons of olive oil in a large skillet. Add vegetable and cook till tender. Stir in the curry powder, cook for an additional 1-2 minutes and turn heat off.

Over a medium high heat, heat a nonstick skillet and then add the remaining oil in which you will fry the eggs.

Serve eggs on top of vegetable

Makes 2 servings

Paleo Diet

PALEO DIET:
SALADS AND SOUPS

Mixed Greens with Almonds and Blueberry Vinaigrette

Takes about 10 minutes to prepare

Ingredients

Dressing

One cup of blueberries

Two tablespoon of water

A quarter cup of white wine vinegar

A quarter cup of olive oil

One teaspoon of thyme

One teaspoon of honey

Salad

Four cups of mixed greens

A quarter cup of almonds (sliced)

Preparation

Put all the dressing ingredients in a blender and blend until smooth. Divide the salad between plates and drizzle with the dressing. Sprinkle almonds on top.

Makes 4 servings

Kale, Cranberry and Sweet Potato Salad

Takes about 20 minutes to prepare

Ingredients

Two bunches of kale (bite-sized pieces)

Three tablespoons of olive oil

Two large sweet potatoes (peeled and cubed)

One teaspoon of Dijon mustard

One tablespoon of lemon juice

A quarter cup of sunflower seeds

Half cup of dried cranberries

Sea salt and fresh ground pepper

Preparation

In a saucepan, place sweet potatoes in and cover with cold water.

Add pinch of salt and bring to boil. Reduce to a simmer until potatoes are soft, this will take 10-15 minutes. Then drain and leave to cool.

Whisk the olive oil, lemon juice and mustard in a large bowl. Add remaining ingredients plus the cooled potatoes. Mix well and serve at room temperature.

Makes 6 servings

Savory Fig Salad

Ingredients

1 pound of fresh figs (quartered)

One tablespoon of olive oil

One teaspoon of chopped rosemary

Honey

Preparation

Slice fresh figs after cleaning and set it aside in a bowl.

Mix the fresh figs with olive oil and fresh rosemary, and drizzle with honey.

Chill it and serve with grilled shrimp skewers, chicken or grilled fish.

Makes 2 servings

Avocado Chicken Salad

Takes about 45 minutes to prepare.

Ingredients

Four chicken thighs (boneless and skinless)

One teaspoon of chili powder

One teaspoon of cumin

One teaspoon of sea salt

One tablespoon of avocado oil

Three avocados

Two tomatoes (small, diced)

Half red onion (diced)

One lime (juice only)

Sea salt and black pepper

Preparation

Preheat the oven to 350^0.

Arrange chicken thighs in a glass baking dish, season with chili powder, cumin and sea salt and drizzle with oil. Add chicken to preheated oven and cook for about 30 minutes (no longer pink). Remove chicken and shred with 2 forks. Set aside to cool. (This can be done ahead of time)

Mash avocado slightly with the back of a fork in a bowl. You want some bits of avocado and some creamy. Add the tomato, onion, and lime juice. Add the chicken. Stir to combine. Season with sea salt and black pepper.

Makes about 4 servings

Coconut Crusted Chicken Salad

Takes about 25 minutes to cook

Ingredients

Two tablespoons of coconut flour

Two chicken fillets

Two tablespoons of unsweetened flaked coconut

One egg (scrambled)

Three tablespoons of apple cider vinegar

Two cups of spring mix salad greens

One teaspoon of honey

Two tablespoons of coconut oil

Three tablespoons of olive oil

Sea salt and black pepper.

Preparation

Make a dredging station with three plates. Add coconut flour to one, egg to the second plate and flaked coconut to the third. Heat the coconut oil in a skillet over medium-high heat. Dredge each chicken fillet in the coconut flour first, followed by the egg, then the flaked coconut, coating each uniformly and coated well. Place each fillet into the hot skillet. Cook on each side (about 5 minutes) until the chicken is golden in color and cooked through. Whisk the apple cider vinegar and honey in a bowl. Continue to whisk while drizzling in the olive oil until well combined and becomes creamy. Season with salt and pepper. Place the spring mix in a mixing bowl. Drizzle the dressing over and mix to coat. Plate the spring mix evenly then serve the chicken on top. Makes 2 servings

Avocado Egg Salad

Ingredients

One egg (Hard-boiled and diced)

Half avocado (diced)

Two slices of cooked bacon (crumbled)

Juice from half a lemon

Sea salt and black pepper

Preparation

Mash avocado slightly and drizzle with lemon juice.

To the avocado, add diced hard-boiled egg. Add bacon and mix together gently. Season with sea salt and black pepper and serve immediately.

Makes 1 serving

Paleo chicken soup

Takes about 30 minutes to prepare

Ingredients

Two cups of cauliflower florets

One cup of chicken breast (cooked and shredded)

Two tablespoons of olive oil

Paprika (one pinch)

Three cups of chicken broth

One teaspoon of thyme

Two stalks of celery (diced)

Two cups of water

Two garlic cloves

One onion (diced)

Sea salt and fresh ground pepper

Preparation

Heat oil in a large saucepan. Add the onion, celery, and garlic and cook for about five minutes.

Add thyme, paprika and cauliflower. Stir, cook for five minutes and add the broth and water.

Bring to boil, reduce heat to a simmer for about 10-15 minutes till cauliflower is tender.

Puree the soup to your liking. Add the chicken to the pot. Serve hot.

Makes 4 servings

Crockpot Sweet Potato Soup with Bacon

Takes about 7 hours to prepare

Ingredients

2 pounds of sweet potatoes (peeled and chopped)

Two cups of chicken stock

One tablespoon of ground cinnamon

One tablespoon of ground nutmeg

One teaspoon of ground ginger

Four slices of bacon (cooked crisply and diced)

Half cup of coconut milk

Preparation

Add sweet potatoes, cinnamon, nutmeg, chicken stock and ginger to crockpot and cook on low for six hours.

Add coconut milk after the six hours. Carefully blend using immersion blender until creamy.

Serve it hot topped with bacon.

Makes about 6 servings

Paleo Diet

PALEO DIET: MAIN MEALS

Paleo Steak and Vegetable Stir-Fry

Takes about 20 minute to prepare

Ingredients

One clove of garlic

Two cups cabbage (shredded)

Half cup shredded carrot

Two tablespoon sesame oil

One pound of sliced steak

One juiced lime

Two green onions (sliced)

Two cups broccoli florets

Preparation

Heat the oil in a big skillet on medium high. Add the green onion, garlic and ginger and cook for a minute or two. Add the steak, cook until turns brown and remove from the skillet.

Stir in the vegetables and cook quickly, continue stirring until veggies are tender. Add the steak back to the pan and add the lime juice.

Cook until heated through and serve.

Make 4 servings

Paleo Italian Meatballs and Braised Greens

Takes about 45 minutes to prepare

Ingredients

Meatballs

One and a half pounds of ground beef

Two tablespoon Italian seasoning

Two tablespoon olive oil

Two cloves garlic (minced)

A quarter cup almond flour

One onion (finely chopped)

Half teaspoon sea salt

One teaspoon paprika

Greens

Four slices bacon (diced)

One bunch collard greens (rinse, remove stems and chop)

Two teaspoon apple cider vinegar

One cup chicken broth (or water)

One bunch of Swiss chard (rinse, remove stems and chop)

Sea salt and fresh ground pepper

Preparation

Preheat oven to 400°F.

Combine the beef, onion, garlic, almond flour, paprika, and salt in a large bowl. Using your hands, mix until just combined, being careful not to over mix. Form into 2-inch meatballs and lay on a baking sheet. Brush with the olive oil and coat with the Italian seasoning. Bake for 20-30 minutes, until cooked through.

To make the greens, cook the bacon a large, deep skillet until it starts to brown. Add the greens and stir to coat in the fat.

Add the broth or water to cover the greens and turn heat down to low. Let the greens simmer for about 10 minutes over low heat, stirring occasionally, until greens are tender. Serve the meatballs over the greens.

Makes 6 servings

Baked Tilapia with Roasted Tomatoes

Takes about 30 minutes to prepare

Ingredients

Two pints cherry tomatoes

A quarter cup olive oil (divided)

Half cup basil leaves (chopped)

One lemon (juiced)

Four tilapia filets

Sea salt and fresh ground pepper

Preparation

Preheat oven to about 400°F

Mix the tomatoes with three tablespoons of olive oil and lay on a parchment lined with baking sheet. Bake it for about 15 minutes till tomatoes blister slightly. Take out of oven and reduce heat to 375°F.

Put the fish filets on another baking sheet and brush filets with rest of olive oil and lemon juice. Season with salt and pepper. Bake for 10 minutes till fish flakes easily with a fork.

Serve the fish topped with the roasted tomatoes and sprinkled with fresh chopped basil.

Makes 4 servings

Paleo Chicken and Cauliflower Stew

Takes about 40 minutes to prepare

Ingredients

Two tablespoons olive oil

Two cloves garlic (minced)

Two cups spinach (chopped)

Two cups cauliflower (cut into florets)

Six cups chicken broth

Half cup coconut milk

Two tablespoons capers

Three chicken breasts

One onion (diced)

Sea salt and fresh ground pepper

Preparation

Heat the oil in a large stockpot or Dutch oven. Add the onions and cook until soft. Add the garlic and cook for another minute.

Stir in the spinach and cauliflower and add the broth. Bring to a boil and add the chicken breasts. Reduce to a simmer and simmer until chicken is cooked, about 20 minutes.

Remove chicken from the pot and shred. Add back to the pot and lightly mash the cauliflower.

Stir in the coconut milk and capers, and simmer until heated through before serving.

Makes 6 servings

Beef and Broccoli

Takes about 20 minutes to prepare

Ingredients

One orange

One cup broccoli (cut into florets)

One round steak (cut into strips)

Half ginger (minced)

Two tablespoons apple cider vinegar

Sea salt and black pepper

Coconut oil

Preparation

Put coconut oil in a medium skillet over medium-high heat.

Add round steak to the skillet and sautés for 3-4 minutes.

Add the broccoli, orange juice, apple cider and ginger.

Season with pepper and salt and continue to sauté until steak is cooked to desired temperature.

Makes 2 servings

Curried Chicken with mashed pumpkin

Takes about one hour to prepare

Ingredients

One pie pumpkin

One teaspoon curry powder

Two tablespoons coconut oil

One clove garlic

One teaspoon grated ginger

Two cups tomato sauce

One onion (diced)

One pound chicken breast (cut in chunks)

Half cup coconut milk

One juice lime

Fresh chopped cilantro

Sea salt and fresh ground pepper

Preparation

Preheat oven to 400°F

Cut the pumpkin in half and scoop out the seeds

Lay on a baking sheet, cut side up. Sprinkle with one teaspoon of coconut oil and season with pepper and salt.

Bake for about 40 minutes fork tender.

Heat remaining coconut oil in a large skillet while the pumpkin is roasting. Add garlic and ginger cook for about 1 minute.

Add onion; cook until soft, add chicken and cook until browned.

Stir in the curry powder, tomato sauce and half the coconut milk. Simmer over medium low heat until sauce is thickened and chicken cooked through Add the lime juice

When the pumpkin is done roasting, remove from oven and allow to cool slightly. Carefully scoop the flesh from the skin and transfer to a bowl. Add the remaining coconut milk and a pinch of salt and pepper and mash the pumpkin with either a fork or potato masher.

Serve with the chicken, and sprinkle with the cilantro.

Makes 4 servings

Maple Mustard Almond Chicken

Takes about 40 minutes to prepare

Ingredients

Two tablespoons Dijon mustard

One tablespoon pure maple syrup

Half teaspoon apple cider vinegar

Half cup almonds (chopped)

Four boneless skinless chicken breast

Sea salt and ground pepper (fresh)

Preparation

Preheat oven to 375°F.

Whisk the mustard, vinegar and maple syrup in a bowl.

Place chopped almonds on a plate. Season the chicken with salt and pepper.

Brush each chicken breast with the mixture and roll in the chopped almonds.

Lay on a baking sheet and bake for 20 to 25 minutes, until chicken is cooked through and browned.

Makes 4 servings

Mustard Crusted Salmon with Arugula and Spinach Salad

Takes about 20 minutes to prepare

Ingredients

Salmon

15 oz of salmon filet

Salt

One tablespoon coarse ground mustard

Salad

One cup arugula

Half cup baby spinach

Two tablespoons pecans (chopped)

Two tablespoons dried cranberries

Dressing

One tablespoon olive oil

One tablespoon white vinegar

One tablespoon Dijon mustard

Preparation

Preheat oven for 350°F

Place the salmon filet on a baking sheet greased with olive oil. Pat dry with a paper towel. Season the salmon with salt and top with the ground mustard, making sure to cover the entire top of the filet.

Place the salmon in the oven and bake for 12 to 15 minutes, until cooked through and flakes easily with a fork.

While the salmon is cooking, whisk together the ingredients for the dressing. Set aside. In a medium mixing bowl combine all the ingredients for the salad. Add the dressing and toss to coat.

Spoon the salad onto a serving plate.

When the salmon is done, remove from the oven. Place it on top of the salad and serve.

Makes 1 serving

Pork Cabbage Rolls

Takes about 40 minute to prepare

Ingredients

Ten savory cabbage leaves

Onion (halved and minced)

1/2 lb of ground pork

One garlic clove (minced)

Two tablespoons coconut aminos

One tablespoon almond meal

Two tablespoons rice vinegar

One egg

Chicken broth

Preparation

Put cabbage in a bowl and pour boiling water on it until totally covered by the water. Leaves it for five minutes, then remove it to cool.

Put the pork, onion, garlic, ginger, coconut aminos, vinegar, almond meal, and egg in another bowl. Mix together with your hands.

Form 10-12 meatball-sized pork balls and set aside. Place each of the pork balls in the center of separate cabbage leaves and wrap ending it underneath.

Pour sufficient chicken broth into a stock pot to reach about 1-inch deep. Place the cabbage rolls in to the pot gently. Cover it with a lid that fits tightly and cook for about 25 minutes in a medium heat.

Serve immediately

Makes 4 servings

Sundried Tomato Roulade

Takes about 40 minutes to prepare

Ingredients

Four turkey cutlets

7-8 sundried tomatoes

Two tablespoons pine nuts

Three tablespoons fresh basil leaves

4 tablespoons olive oil

Sea salt (half teaspoon)

Sea salt and black pepper

Preparation

Preheat oven to 350⁰F

Toast the pine nuts in a skillet over a medium-high heat for about five minutes. Make sure they don't stick nor burn.

Blend sundried tomatoes, basil, toasted pine nuts and salt together in a food processer. Pour in olive oil while blending.

Spread sundried tomato mixture on the surface of salt-seasoned cutlet. Roll cutlet tightly and pin with a toothpick.

Put coconut oil in an oven proof medium skillet over medium high heat and add each roulade until each side is browned. In order not to damage the meat, use soft tipped tongs to turn.

Then cook in the preheated oven for about 10 minutes. Cut into roulade discs and season.

Makes 4 servings

Chicken Lettuce Wraps

Takes about 30 minutes to prepare

Ingredients

1 lb of chicken tenders (diced in to about 1 inch pieces)

One onion (diced)

One garlic clove (minced)

6-7 white mushrooms (diced)

One orange pepper (diced)

3 carrots (sliced)

3 celery stalks (diced)

5-6 brussels sprouts (stem set aside and quartered)

One tablespoon coconut aminos

Two tablespoons coconut oil

One teaspoon red pepper flake

One head iceberg lettuce

Sea salt and black pepper

Preparation

Heat coconut oil in a large skillet over medium heat and add celery, onion, garlic, mushrooms, carrots, orange pepper and brussels sprouts. Sauté for about 5 minutes. Add chicken and sauté for another five minutes until it begins to brown. Stir frequently. Add rice vinegar, ground ginger, coconut aminos and crushed red pepper flake. Stir to coat. Season with salt and pepper. Sauté for another 3 minutes for chicken to cook through. Put in a serving plate with the iceberg lettuce.

To eat, spoon about 2 tablespoons of the chicken mixture in to a lettuce leaf, fold over and eat. Makes 4 servings

Lemon and Thyme Roasted Chicken Breast

Takes about 35 minutes to prepare

Ingredients

Two chicken breasts with bones and skin removed

One lemon

7 sprigs of thyme (stem not needed)

One tablespoon olive oil (more needed for sprinkling)

Salt and pepper

Preparation

Place chicken in a sealable bag container. Squeeze lemon over the chicken.

Add thyme and olive oil. Toss to coat and season with salt. Set aside in the refrigerator at least 40 minutes and could be up to 8 hours.

Preheat oven to 350^0F then sprinkle olive oil on the chicken in a baking dish and bake for about 30 minutes.

Pepper to taste and serve

Makes 2 servings

Beef Vindaloo

Ingredients

Beef

One and a half lbs Beef Stew meat (diced into 2 inch pieces)

One third cup red wine vinegar

Two tablespoons olive oil

One teaspoon sea salt

Vindaloo

Two tablespoons olive oil

One onion (finely sliced)

Half onion (chopped)

Four garlic cloves (minced)

One tablespoon ground ginger

Half teaspoon ground mustard

Half teaspoon ground cumin

One teaspoon turmeric

One teaspoon cayenne pepper

Half teaspoon ground coriander

One teaspoon paprika

Half teaspoon ground cinnamon

Six oz tomato paste

One cup beef stock

One large tomato (diced)

One tablespoon red wine vinegar

One bay leaf

Half lb sweet potatoes (cut into 1 inch cubes)

Sea salt

Black pepper

Preparation

In a bowl, mix together red wine vinegar, olive oil, and sea salt. Add the diced meat and mix to coat. Wrap with plastic wrap and place in the refrigerator overnight to marinate (or at least 8 hours).

Preheat the oven to 350⁰F.

Blend the half chopped onion, four garlic cloves, ground ginger, turmeric, ground mustard, ground cumin, cayenne pepper, paprika, ground coriander, and ground cinnamon in a food processor until it forms a paste. Set aside.

Heat one tablespoon of olive oil in an oven safe deep skillet over medium high heat. Drain the marinade from the beef.

Add the beef to the pan in two batches and brown, about 3-4 minutes per side. Remove from the pan and set aside.

Lower heat to medium. Add the sliced onions and cook until they become translucent, about 5-7 minutes.

Add the spice paste and cook for 1-2 minutes, stirring frequently until the spices become fragrant. Add the tomato paste and cook for another 2 minutes, stir frequently.

Add the beef stock and stir well to combine all the ingredients.

Add the beef back to the pan. Add the tomatoes, red wine vinegar, bay leaf, and sweet potatoes. Transfer the entire pan to the oven and bake for 60 minutes.

After 60 minutes, remove from the oven. Season with salt and pepper. Serve. Makes about 2 servings

Italian Sausage and Peppers

Takes about 30 minutes to prepare

Ingredients

Four Italian sausages (fully cooked) or chicken sausage

One red onion

One tablespoon coconut oil

Two bell peppers (sliced in to strips)

Sea salt and black pepper

Preparation

Heat oil in a skillet over medium heat

Add the sausages and cook for about 5 minutes. Turn it often in order to ensure even browning. Then move to it to a side in the skillet and add pepper and sliced onion. Sauté onion and pepper until soft.

Slice each sausage to 4-5 slices on a cutting board.

Transfer the onions and peppers to a serving plate and top with sausage.

Season with sea salt and black pepper.

Makes 4 servings

Almond Pesto Crusted Cod with Pesto Zucchini Noodles

Takes about 15 minutes to prepare

Ingredients

Pesto

Two cups arugula

Three tablespoons sliced almonds

Half lemon (juiced)

A quarter cup olive oil

Salt

Noodles

One zucchini (spiraled into noodle shape)

One tablespoon olive oil

A quarter cup cherry tomatoes

A quarter cup pesto

Salt

Cod

Two tablespoons ground almonds

Two tablespoons pesto

5 oz cod

Salt

Preparation

Preheat oven to 350°F. Blend the ingredients for the pesto in a blender or food processor until smooth and set aside. Mix two tablespoons of both the ground almonds and pesto in a bowl.

Pat the piece of cod dry with a paper towel. Season fish with salt and place on a baking sheet. Spoon the pesto and almond paste on top of the fish, press it down a bit to form a crust.

Bake fish in oven for about 10 minutes. While fish is baking, heat oil over medium heat and add zucchini noodles together with a quarter cup of pesto. Sauté until noodles are tender and season with salt.

Spoon noodles onto a plate and place the baked fish over it, garnish with cherry tomatoes.

Makes 1 serving

Sweet potato and chicken curry

Ingredients

1 lb chicken breast (cut into 1 inch chunks)

Two tablespoons olive oil

Two sweet potatoes (cut in 1 inch pieces)

Half onion

Two garlic cloves

One tablespoon curry powder

One tablespoon ground ginger

One can coconut milk

Half cup chicken stock

Salt and black pepper

Preparation

Heat one tablespoon of cooking oil in a skillet over medium heat.

Add the chicken breast chunks and season with pepper and salt. Brown the chicken, 3-4 minute for each side.

Set chicken aside when cooked and add remaining one tablespoon of oil to the pan. Add onions; cook until translucent, 5-7 minutes.

Add ground ginger, garlic and curry powder then cook for another 1-2 minutes.

Add chicken stock and deglaze the pan; scrape all the brown bits off the bottom of the pan.

Add coconut milk and sweet potatoes. Put the chicken back in the pan.

Simmer until the sweet potatoes are tender; 17-20 minutes. Season with pepper and salt.

Makes 4 servings

Twice Baked Sweet Potato

Ingredients

Two sweet potatoes

One cup chicken (cooked and shredded)

Sea salt

Coconut oil

1/3 cup fresh green onions (diced)

Avocado

Hot sauce (optional garnish)

Preparation

Preheat oven to 350^0F. Poke sweet potatoes all over using a fork and slather some coconut oil onto the skins with your hands. Sprinkle with sea salt lightly and cook for one hour.

When potatoes are cooked, cut open and stuff with shredded chicken. Put back in oven until middle is warmed through.

Garnish with sliced avocado, fresh chopped green onion and hot sauce if desired.

Makes 2 servings

Cashew Chicken

Takes about 30 minutes to cook

Ingredients

Two boneless and skinless chicken breasts

One red bell pepper and one onion (both cut into strips)

One garlic cloves (minced)

Half cup raw chopped cashews

One tablespoon coconut amino

Two tablespoons coconut oil

One tablespoon rice vinegar

Two tablespoons honey

One teaspoon fresh grated ginger

Three scallions

Black pepper and sea salt

Preparation

Heat coconut oil in a skillet over medium heat, add red pepper and onion, and cook for few minutes. Season each side of chicken with salt and pepper. Add the chicken to the onions and bell pepper and cook for about 5 minutes each side.

Add the garlic and cashews, mix and cook for another 3 minutes.

Stir in the rice vinegar, coconut amino, grated ginger, honey and season with pepper and salt. Cook for another 4-5 minutes.

Serve and garnish with scallions.

Makes 4 servings

Beef Stew

Ingredients

1.5 lbs beef stew meat

One cup onion

Three tablespoons garlic (minced)

8 oz mushrooms (sliced)

Three tablespoons coconut oil (divided)

One tablespoon balsamic vinegar

One inch sweet potato (cut into 1 chunks)

Two stems diced celery

One bay leaf

Four cups beef broth (divided)

Two tablespoons arrowroot powder

One teaspoon garlic powder

Pepper and sea salt

Preparation

Melt 1 Tablespoons of coconut oil in a large Dutch oven and lightly sauté onion and garlic.

Prepare your stew meat by sprinkling with garlic powder, sea salt, and fresh cracked pepper. Make sure it is uniformly coated on all sides.

As the onions and garlic are warming, heat up a skillet that you will use to sear the meat. Melt 1 tablespoon of coconut oil in the skillet (reserve the remaining tablespoon of coconut oil for the mushrooms).

Once the skillet is nice and hot, place stew meat in the pan and sear on each side for about 45 seconds. Remove from heat and add stew meat to Dutch oven with the onions and garlic.

Add 3 cups of the beef broth to the Dutch oven and turn to low.

Add cubed sweet potato, celery, and bay leaf to the Dutch oven. Stir to combine. Using the sauté pan that you used to sear the meat, warm the tablespoon of coconut oil left and toss in the mushrooms, being sure to scrape up any pan drippings. Turn heat to medium and warm mushrooms until they begin to soften (3-5 minutes).

While mushrooms are cooking, take two tablespoons of arrowroot powder and put into a small mason jar. Fill mason jar with remaining cup of beef broth. Screw lid on tight and shake vigorously until the arrowroot powder is dissolved.

Stir mushrooms with 1 tablespoon of balsamic vinegar, making sure that they are all evenly coated.

Add arrowroot/broth mixture to the pan with the mushrooms and stir constantly until the broth turns into a thick gravy.

Once the mushrooms and gravy are thickened, pour the entire contents into the Dutch oven with the rest of the soup.

Bring the soup to a low simmer and simmer for 2 hours, stirring occasionally. Depending on the type of stew meat you've used, longer cooking times may be required to soften the meat. If the meat is tough, you probably need to simmer the stew longer.

Serve hot.

Makes 6 servings

Buffalo Chicken Poppers

Ingredients

Six mini peppers (halved, seeds and ribs removed)

One cup chicken (cooked, shredded)

Three tablespoons onion (diced)

Two hard boiled eggs (diced)

Sauce

½ cup hot sauce

2 ½ tablespoons ghee

One tablespoon coconut aminos

One teaspoon apple cider vinegar

½ teaspoon garlic powder

¼ teaspoon cayenne pepper (optional)

Preparation

To make sauce, place a small saucepan over medium heat. Add all ingredients in the pan. Once ghee is melted, whisk to combine. Set aside. Mix shredded chicken, onion, and hardboiled eggs together in a bowl. Use 1-2 tablespoons of sauce (or how much you like) over chicken mixture and combine well. Spoon chicken mixture into pepper halves. Place on baking pan. Bake at 325°F for about 30 minutes.

Transfer unused sauce into a glass jar with lid and store in fridge for up to 2 weeks.

Egg baked in Acorn Squash

Takes about 60 minutes to prepare.

Ingredients

 One acorn squash (cut in half and deseeded)

Two eggs

One tablespoon fresh chives (chopped)

Salt and black pepper

Preparation

Preheat oven to 375^{0}F.

Place the squash face down on a parchment lined baking sheet. Bake the squash in the oven for 25-35 minutes, until the squash becomes soft. Pierce with fork to see if tender. Take out of oven and allow to cool slightly, about 5 minutes.

Place the squash halves face up on the baking sheet. Crack an egg into the hole in each half. Season with salt and pepper. Bake in the oven for 15 to 20 minutes until the egg sets.

Take out of the oven and garnish with fresh chives and serve.

Makes 2 servings

Mini Paleo Meatloaves

Takes about 45 minutes to prepare

Ingredients

Mini Meatloaves

1 lb turkey

One tablespoon olive oil

¼ onion (minced)

¼ cup carrots (diced fine)

1/4 cup green pepper (diced fine)

1/4 teaspoon marjoram

1/4 teaspoon thyme

One egg

1/4 teaspoon salt

1/4 teaspoon black pepper

¼ cup Paleo ketchup

Paleo Ketchup

6 oz tomato paste

1/4 cup honey

½ cup white wine vinegar

1/4 cup water

3/4 teaspoon salt

1/8 teaspoon onion powder

1/8 teaspoon garlic powder

Preparation

Preheat oven to 350⁰F.

Heat the olive oil in a skillet over medium heat. Add the onions, carrots and green peppers and cook until translucent, about 3-5 minutes. Transfer the ingredients into a bowl and add the ground turkey, marjoram, thyme, egg, and salt and pepper.

Mix the ingredients together very well with your hands.

Form the meat mixture into about 10 separate loaves and set them on a foil lined baking sheet.

Whisk together the ingredients for the paleo ketchup in another bowl and spread some on top of each of the separate meatloaves.

Put meatloaves in the oven and bake for about 25 minutes, until cooked through.

Serve warm

Makes 4 servings

Mini Steak Bites

Ingredients

1 lb beef stew meat (pre-cut)

Sea salt and freshly ground pepper

Four tablespoons ghee

Preparation

Prepare pieces of meat by removing fat and gristle and cut it into 1-2 inch chunks.

Sprinkle meat pieces with sea salt and freshly cracked peppercorns. Roll around to coat well.

Melt two tablespoons of ghee in a heated skillet. Stir until browned. NOTE: will be smoky.

Once pan is sizzling, add the steak bites and cook each side for about 50 seconds.

Remove from heat immediately and place on a nice serving platter.

Add remaining two tablespoons of ghee to the drippings in the pan and leave to melt. Pour this sauce into a bowl for dipping.

Serve with toothpicks to turn bites into finger food, if desire.

Makes 2 servings

Pesto Stuffed Sardines

Takes about 20 minutes

Ingredient

Pesto

Two cups fresh spinach (packed)

One garlic clove

1/4 cup almonds

Two tablespoons of olive oil

Salt

Sardines

Six Fresh sardines

Two tablespoons coconut oil (melted)

Salt

Black pepper

Preparation

Preheat the broiler. Place the top rack about five inches from the top of the broiler.

Blend all ingredients for pesto in a blender or food procesor until a paste is formed and set aside.

Rinse sardines, dry with paper towel and place on a foil lined baking sheet.

Stuff each sardine with one tablespoon of the pesto and brush the sides of the sardine with coconut oil, then season with salt and pepper.

Cook each side of the sardine for 4 minutes in a broiler until cooked through. Serve.

Makes 4 servings

Paleo Sloppy Joes

Takes about 20 minutes

Ingredient

1 lb ground beef (turkey is a good option too)

One bell pepper (diced)

One onion (diced)

One teaspoon cumin

Three celery stalks (diced)

One garlic clove (minced)

¼ teaspoon red pepper flake (optional)

One teaspoon chili powder

¼ teaspoon cayenne pepper (optional)

Two cups tomato sauce

Fresh cracked black pepper

Two tablespoons coconut oil

Sea salt

Preparation

Heat coconut oil over medium heat in a skillet. Add the onion, celery and pepper and sauté for about 5 minutes.

Add garlic, sauté for about 1 minute and add the ground beef and cook until browned and thoroughly.

Stir in tomato sauce and spices.

Cook on medium heat (about 10 minutes) until sauce thickens a bit. Serve hot.

Makes 4 servings

Chicken Taco Bar

Ingredients

Six chicken breasts or thighs (cooked and shredded)

Half cup chicken broth

Half teaspoon chili powder

Half teaspoon ground cumin

1/8 teaspoon cayenne pepper

¼ teaspoon ground mustard

Half teaspoon garlic powder

¼ teaspoon onion powder

Half teaspoon dried oregano

Half teaspoon sea salt

Two tomatoes diced

14-16 Romaine leaves

Topping Options

Half cup carrot (shredded)

One onion (diced)

Half cup cabbage (shredded)

4-6 slices of bacon (cooked crispy and crumbled)

1-2 avocados (diced)

One cup of Broccoli (shredded or diced)

1-2 Jalapeno (diced)

Preparation

Add cooked chicken to a sauce pan plus the chicken broth on medium low heat.

Stir in chili powder, cumin, cayenne, ground mustard, garlic powder, onion powder, oregano, and salt.

Cook until chicken is heated through and broth thickened.

Place warm chicken in a serving bowl. Place each topping items in individual serving bowls. Stack the romaine lettuce leaves on a plate for serving. To serve: place romaine lettuce on plate, top with chicken, add favorite toppings. Enjoy!

Makes 6 servings

Slow Cooker Carne Asada

Ingredients

2 lbs sirloin steaks boneless

1/4 oz green chiles (diced)

Two onions (diced)

Three tomatoes (roughly chopped)

Three garlic cloves (minced)

One jalapeno (seeded and diced)

One tablespoon cumin

One red bell pepper (diced)

¼ teaspoon red pepper flake

Two tablespoons chili powder

¼ teaspoon cayenne

Sea salt and black pepper

1/3 cup beef broth

8-10 romaine leaves

Preparation

Season the steak with salt and pepper then add half the onion to the bottom of the slow cooker.

Place the steak on top of the onion and add remaining onion, tomato, green chilies, garlic, jalapeno, cumin, red bell pepper, red pepper flakes, chili powder, cayenne, salt and pepper.

Pour in the beef broth. Gently stir to combine.

Set the slow cooker for 6-7 hours on low and when it's about 45 minutes left, remove steak, shred with forks and return to the slow cooker to complete the cooking. Serve in a romaine lettuce leaf. Makes 4 servings.

Chorizo Burger

Ingredients

Burger

1 lb ground beef (at room temperature)

1 lb chorizo (casings removed, at room temperature)

Topping

Two avocados (diced)

One red onion (diced)

Two tomatoes (medium, diced)

One lime (juiced)

Sea salt

Black pepper

Preparation

Preheat the oven to 400^{0}F.

Use parchment paper to line a rimmed baking sheet.

Combine the beef and chorizo very well in a bowl with your hands. Form the combined meat into patties of equal sizes.

Place the patties on the lined baking sheet and cook in a preheated oven until cooked through, about 20 minutes.

While the burgers are cooking, make topping by combining the avocado, onion, and tomato.

Add the lime juice and stir to coat.

Season with sea salt and black pepper and top each burger with the topping mixture.

Makes about 6 servings

Paleo Vension Burgers

Ingredients

1 lb ground venison meat

One tablespoon onion powder

One tablespoon garlic powder

1/2 cup parsley (fresh chopped)

Sea salt and pepper

One cup onion (sliced)

One tablespoon balsamic vinegar

One tablespoon coconut oil or olive oil

Preparation

Combine ground venison with onion powder, garlic powder, chopped parsley, salt and pepper in a bowl. Use your hands to combine everything well and form the mixture into 4-5 patties. Set aside. Heat the oil in a large pan on medium high. Once the pan is nice and hot, add the burgers, cover them, and cook them for about 3-4 minutes on each side. Once the first side is cooked and you're ready to turn, add the sliced onions to the pan to cook along with the burgers. Watch very well and stir the onions as necessary to avoid getting burnt. Continue to cook onions till caramelized. Once everything is cooked through, remove burgers from the pan and turn off the heat. Add one tablespoon of balsamic vinegar to the onions left in the pan and deglaze the pan and drippings with the vinegar. Combine well with the onions. Spoon caramelized onions and "gravy" over the top of the burgers and serve hot with fresh steamed veggies. Makes 4 servings

Open Faced Portobello Sandwich

Takes about 10 minutes

Ingredients

Two portobello mushrooms (wiped cleaned with damp paper towel)

Four slices of bacon (cooked)

Two tablespoons olive oil

Two cups baby spinach

One avocado (pitted and sliced)

One lemon (juiced)

Sea salt and pepper.

Preparation

Preheat broiler to high heat. Brush mushroom with olive oil and season with salt and pepper. Lay on a baking sheet and broil for about 5 minutes until lightly browned. Take out of oven and let it cool slightly.

Top each mushroom with half of spinach, avocado and bacon. Drizzle with the lemon juice before serving.

Makes 2 servings

Paleo Diet

PALEO DIET: DESSERTS

Dark Chocolate Hazelnut Brownies

Takes about 30 minutes to prepare

Ingredients

4 oz hazelnuts

4 oz unsweetened chocolate (chopped)

1/4 teaspoon sea salt

1/4 teaspoon baking soda

One teaspoon vanilla extract

1/2 cup coconut oil

1/2 cup dates

Three eggs

Preparation

Preheat oven to 350^0F

Process hazelnuts until you have a flour like texture. Be careful not to over process.

Add salt, baking soda and chopped chocolate and pulse until you have a sandy texture.

Add the dates and pulse until well combined, then add the eggs, coconut oil and vanilla. At this point, it should be thick and smooth.

Pour the batter into a square baking dish and bake for about 20 minutes or until a toothpick inserted in the center comes out clean.

Once cooled, cut into squares and serve.

Frozen Fruit Kabob with Paleo Fruit Dip

Takes about 20 minutes to prepare

Ingredients

Two cups fruit cut into evenly sized pieces (pineapple, cantaloupe, watermelon, honey dew, etc.)

Eight strawberries hulled

Four blueberries

One cup coconut milk (full fat)

Two tablespoon of honey

One banana frozen

Pinch nutmeg fresh

Four wooden skewers

Preparation

Make kabobs by adding fruit to each in a uniform pattern; example- strawberry, blueberry, watermelon, cantaloupe and top with another strawberry. Make four.

Place kabobs in airtight bag and freeze for minimum of 4 hours or over the night.

To prepare fruit dip; blend coconut milk, honey and frozen banana until frothy and smooth.

Transfer to a serving bowl, top with nutmeg. Serve kabob with the dip by it.

Makes 4 servings

No Bake Chocolate Chips Cookies

Takes about 10 minutes to prepare

Ingredients

One cup of almond butter

1/4 cup ground flax seed

Half cup dark chocolate chips

1/4 cup coconut oil (melted)

Half cup coconut flakes (unsweetened)

Sea salt to taste

Preparation

Mix all ingredients in a bowl ensuring they are well combined. Use a cookie scoop to scoop onto parchment. Chill until ready to serve.

Lemon Bars

Takes about 15 minutes to prepare

Ingredients

Crust

One cup almond flour

¼ cup almond butter

one tablespoon honey

one tablespoon coconut oil (plus more for coating pan)

one teaspoon vanilla

½ teaspoon baking powder

¼ teaspoon sea salt

Filling

Three eggs

½ cup honey

¼ cup lemon juice

2 ½ tablespoon coconut flour

one tablespoon lemon zest, finely grated

Pinch of sea salt

Preparation

Preheat oven to 350⁰F. Coat 9x9 baking dish with coconut oil. Combine all crust ingredients in food processor and pulse until a "crumble" forms. Press crust evenly into the bottom of baking dish. Using a fork, prick a few holes into the crust. Bake for 10 minutes. While crust is baking, combine all filling ingredient in a food processor and blend until well incorporated. Remove crust from oven when done and pour filling evenly over top. Bake for 15-20 minutes or until filling is set, but still has a little jiggle. Cool completely on wire rack. You can also chill in the fridge if desired to further set the filling.

Paleo Chocolate Cake

Takes about 30 minutes to prepare

Ingredients

Cake

3/4 cup coconut flour

¼ cup arrowroot starch

2/3 cup cocoa powder

one teaspoon baking powder

¾ teaspoon sea salt

seven large eggs (room temperature)

ten tablespoon ghee (melted)

two teaspoon vanilla

¾ cup plus 2 tablespoon maple syrup

¼ cup canned coconut milk

Ganache

12 oz Paleo approved chocolate chips

2/3 cup canned coconut milk

4 tablespoon ghee

Preparation

Preheat oven to 350⁰F. Line the bottoms of two 6" round baking pans with parchment circles. Grease and flour (use arrowroot or tapioca flour) the sides of the pan. In a mixing bowl, mix together the coconut flour, arrowroot flour, cocoa powder, baking powder and salt. Set aside. In a large mixing bowl, beat the eggs together. Add in the butter, vanilla, and maple syrup, mix until smooth and well combined. Add half of the egg mixture to the dry ingredients and mix together well, until no lumps remain. Pour the rest of the egg mixture in and mix until smooth. Add the coconut milk and mix until smooth. Divide the batter between the two prepared pans, smoothing the tops out. Making the sides of the batter higher than the center (this will help it to even out while cooking). Bake for 40 minutes or until a toothpick inserted in the center of the cake comes out clean. Remove from oven and cool pans on a wire rack for 10 minutes. Remove the cakes from the pans and allow finishing cooling on the racks.

To make the ganache; place the chocolate chips, coconut milk and ghee in a microwave safe bowl and heat in microwave for 1 minute. Stir and microwave again for 30 seconds. Whisk until smooth. Microwave 30 seconds more if needed. Let the ganache sit for about 45 minutes to thicken up a bit. Once ganache is set and cakes are cooled completely, level the tops of the cakes if needed. Place one cake on a serving platter and top with ½ cup of ganache. Smooth until top is covered. Place the second cake on top of the first cake. Frost the top and sides with the remaining ganache. Serve at room temperature or chilled.

Energy Bites

Ingredients

Two cups pitted dates

One cup almonds

Two tablespoons almond butter

One tablespoon unsweetened almond milk

Two tablespoons cocoa powder

½ teaspoon vanilla

¼ teaspoon salt

¼ cup unsweetened shredded coconut (optional)

Preparations

Line a baking pan with wax paper, set aside. (You will not be baking these, you just need a place to set your rolled bites as you make them).

Put dates and almonds in your food processor. Process until mixture is fine and uniform.

Add the almond butter, almond milk, cocoa powder, vanilla and salt to your food processor and process until mixture just starts to clump together. Mix in shredded coconut if desire.

Scoop 1 tablespoon portions of your dough, roll into balls in the palm of your hand and place them on your prepared baking sheet. Put them in the fridge for 30 minutes or freezer for 15 minutes. Transfer to an airtight container. These can be stored at room temperature, but will last longer when kept in the fridge or freezer.

Paleo Granola Bars

Takes about 10 to prepare

Ingredients

2 cups chopped pecans

1 cup chopped walnuts

1 cup chopped almonds

20 dates finely chopped

3/4 cup egg whites (from box of egg whites)

2 tablespoons cinnamon

1 1/2 teaspoons vanilla

Preparations

Preheat the oven to 350°F degrees.

In a large bowl, mix together all of the ingredients.

To prepare the 9x13 pan, line it with parchment paper or

aluminum foil and spray it with cooking spray. Press the nut mixture into the bottom of the pan evenly.

Bake for 16-18 minutes. Allow the bars to cool for 5 minutes then pull on the wax paper to remove them from the pan. Slice the bars into rectangles of the size you'd like.

Vanilla Cupcakes

Takes about 20 minutes to prepare

Ingredients

Cupcakes

2 ½ cups almond flour

¼ cup melted coconut oil

1 tablespoon almond milk

½ cup honey

4 large eggs

½ teaspoon baking powder

½ teaspoon sea salt

Two tablespoons vanilla extract

Frosting

One cup raw cashews (soaked for at least 4 hours, drained well and rinsed)

Two tablespoons coconut oil (melted)

1/4 cup honey

2 ½ tablespoon water

¼ teaspoon lemon juice

one tablespoon vanilla extract

pinch of sea salt

Preparations

Make the frosting a day ahead. Place all the ingredients except water in a high power blender or food processor and blend until smooth. Add the water, a tablespoon at the time until the filling become silky and you get your desired texture. Place a sealed container and chill in the refrigerator overnight.

To make the cupcakes, preheat oven to 350°F.

Line a 12-cup muffin pan with paper cups. In a large bowl combine the almond flour, salt and baking powder. In a small bowl combine the eggs, almond milk, honey and vanilla. Stir in the melted coconut oil. Stir egg mixture into almond flour mixture and mix well until combine. Spoon the batter into the paper liners. Bake for about 20 minutes until risen and a toothpick inserted in the center of the cake comes out clean. Remove from the oven, transfer to a wire rack and leave to cool completely.

Transfer the frosting to a pastry bag and pipe it onto the cupcakes using your favorite tip. Enjoy!

PALEO DIET: SMOOTHIES

Primal Green Smoothie

Ingredients

3 tablespoons of 100% liquid egg whites

1/2 cup fresh mint, torn

1 avocado

1 ½ cups organic baby kale

3 *tangerines/mandarin oranges*

6 ice cubes

1/2 cup water

Preparation

Add all the ingredients to a blender. If there's too much ice it may be thicker than you'd like so add some water and blend again. Continue to do so until it's the right consistency. Pour into a glass, and serve.

Sour Cherry Smoothie

Ingredients

¼ cup honey

1 cup water

1 cup sour cherries (frozen)

1 banana (frozen)

1 lemon (juiced)

Preparation

Blend all ingredients until smooth and serve immediately.

Banana Paleo Smoothie

Ingredients

3 bananas (frozen)

1 (13.5 oz) can of coconut milk

1-2 cups of ice

1 tablespoon of collagen peptides (optional)

Preparation

Add peeled bananas, the entire can of coconut milk and the ice to a blender. Use the chop setting to break up the ice, then process until smooth. If you have it, add collagen peptides for a little extra boost of protein and blend to combine well. Divide the smoothie between two glasses and serve. Makes 2-3 servings

Chocolate Peppermint Chia Smoothie

Ingredients

2 bananas (frozen)

2 tablespoons unsweetened cocoa powder

1 cup almond milk

1 tablespoon chia seeds

½ teaspoon peppermint extract.

Preparation

Blend all ingredients until smooth and creamy. Serve immediately.

Makes two servings

Blackberry Coconut Smoothie

Ingredients

1 cup blackberries (frozen)

1 teaspoon coconut oil

½ cup coconut milk

1 banana (frozen)

Preparation

Blend all ingredients until smooth and serve.

Banana-Pear Green Smoothie

Ingredients

2 bananas (frozen)

2 ripe organic pears

1 - 2 cups organic baby spinach (washed)

1 cucumber

¼ -1/2 cup of egg whites

4 – 5 ice cubes

Preparation

Peal and add the bananas to the bottom of the blender. Slice the pear into three to four large pieces, cutting away from the core & seeds in the center. Wash and chop off the ends of the cucumber and add in two to three chunks to the blender. Add spinach to the top. Blend on pulse to chop everything. Blend until smooth and then add the ice. Pour in a glass and serve.

Paleo Green Fig and Mint Smoothie

Ingredients

1 Persian cucumber (ends trimmed)

2 bananas (frozen)

4 fresh green or black figs

1 full tablespoon almond butter

1 cup organic baby kale

1 cup organic baby spinach

5-6 sprigs fresh mint

½ to 1 cup of water

4 -6 ice cubes

Preparation

Add all ingredients, except the ice, to a blender in the order listed, starting with ½ cup of water. By adding the ingredients in this order the blade will hit the harder vegetables first and break them down. You may need to stop the blade and use a wooden spoon to mix everything around to incorporate the lighter greens to meet the blade.

Mix until smooth, adding more water if necessary for your preferred consistency. Add the ice and blitz until chopped and combined. Pour into two glasses and serve.

FINAL WORD

There are a number of diets floating around under the name "Paleo," I am not specifically referring to anyone but I believe you can correctly judge them based on what you have learned. In addition, I have come across many arguments both for and against the paleo diet, and a lot of misinformation on both sides and I believe that if you have read this book up to this point, you know enough to help you stand your ground and even convince others. I tried as much as possible not to be too technical so that almost anyone can digest this material.

Conclusively, in following the above guidelines, do not be an extremist and at the same time do not compromise and I am far too sure that the results will be unfathomable! PALEO DIET IS SUCH A GREAT DIET!

Made in the USA
Columbia, SC
23 December 2018